About the Author

Waldek, 1916

Walde[...] [...]s
born i[...]

His tra[...] [...]ne early on in his life due the Bolshevik invasion of Poland in 1920 and continued with the combined German and Russian invasions at the start of World War II. He arrived in Britain in 1940 where his contribution to the Allied war effort as a pilot in the Polish Air Force (304 Squadron, Coastal Command) earned him the rank of Major.

At the end of the war Waldek decided to make Britain his home and has held British citizenship for over 60 years. He has spent most of this time at his home in Devon and lectured in Further Education, teaching Mechanical Engineering Science.

Waldek was married for 55 years to Dorothy and has two children, John and Vanda.

Three Escapes and a Final Capture

A Young Polish Airman's Wartime Adventures

To Pat

by

Waldemar Josef Siewruk

Siewruk
('Valdek)

Valdek
died
CHRISTMAS EVE
2008
(AGED) 93 yrs
A lovely man

Published 2005 by arima publishing

www.arimapublishing.com

ISBN 1-84549-086-X

Printed and bound in the United Kingdom

Typeset in Palatino Linotype 11/14

The two Europe maps that appear on pages 80 and 81 are printed courtesy of Adrian Chapman, www.adrianchapman.com.

swirl is an imprint of arima Publishing

arima publishing
ASK House, Northgate Avenue
Bury St Edmunds, Suffolk IP32 6BB
t: (+44) 01284 700321
www.arimapublishing.com

For Dorothy.
Without whose love and devotion this
book would never have been written.

Prologue

What I would like to say first of all is that without the great help from my son John and the "editorial reading" by my six very kind neighbours and friends "My Story" would really never have been finished.

John helped me to advance from the typewriter to the word processor, which was his by the way and without which I would still be discovering errors of all kinds and retyping page after page.

I don't know whether one ever reaches the stage of complete satisfaction with one's written work. There always is something that could have been stated in better words or in not so many words and so on.

My first reader was my dear wife who not only read it but also urged me to "get on with it" when I left it alone for too long.

So I am very grateful to my darling wife, to my very dear son John and to all my excellent friends – the neighbours.

Bolshevik Invasion - 1920

When I was four and half years old there were five of us in the family. I now had a younger brother and also a little sister only a few months old. I had been born in Minsk and we now lived in a village near to Pinsk, on the bank of the River Prypec to the south east of the City.

The months of snow were over and spring was in full swing. The river was still very wide but the floods had started to recede and the fields were slowly drying out. Every living thing was looking forward to another summer but in my family something felt not quite normal.

Somehow I could not help feeling that my parents were not in their usual happy mood. My mother very rarely sang or even hummed and my father had given up whistling. Occasionally I heard them discussing something in agitated voices as if they were arguing. This worried me even more when, if I ran into the house, I would find them suddenly quiet and looking at me with eyes full of anxiety. I could not understand this at all. At other times when I appeared unexpectedly in the kitchen I would find my mother in tears for no reason that I could see. Even more unusual was the fact that my father was occasionally away from home for a few days and nights. It was only much later that I discovered that he and some other men from the village had had to go into hiding.

Not many days later I found my mother, not in her usual routine but in tears and rather hurriedly putting together a very disorganised breakfast. Immediately after the hurried meal Ivdokya, our maid, took my sister Olenka in her arms and asked my brother Genio to follow her. This was not the usual time for our walk or play in the garden. Being the eldest of the "trio" I was allowed to either go with the maid or to stay close to the house. This time I decided to dash in after only a few minutes outside. To my astonishment I found my parents frantically packing some of our possessions. I stared at them and at the two men rushing about and carrying out bundles, boxes and cases down to the river. I followed them and found them loading everything into a large rowing boat.

I liked that river and the boats...it usually meant fun for me but on this occasion my parents followed us to the boat carrying our belongings. It was beyond my comprehension why my parents had grim faces and why our maid, standing by the path, was crying softly and rocking Olenka on one arm. She was also pressing Genio into the folds of her capacious skirt, as if she was trying to hide and protect him.

One more trip of the "loading party" and all of us, including Ivdokya and the two men, scrambled into the boat and found seats amongst all those bundles, boxes and treasures which my parents deemed indispensable. Mother held Olenka in her arms, Genio was on Ivdokya's knees and I was wedged safely between two bundles of bedding. Father was rearranging things to make his beloved gramophone more comfortable and secure. Its huge horn looked like the head of an enormous flower, laid to rest on top of a heap of soft stuff. Father loved music and could produce a melody on an instrument quite unknown to him after only a few minutes of testing and tinkling. He could out-whistle blackbirds and robins...even canaries.

I was quite close to the edge of the boat and had no difficulty to trail my hand in the water. It showed how badly overloaded we were. I was enjoying myself when suddenly we heard shots fired behind us and could see splashes in the water not far away. The rhythm of rowing became frantic and the shots, mixed with shouts, were heard not very far away from us. Luckily neither our boat nor anyone in it was hit.

By now we were not far from our landing point and we reached it only a few minutes later. Somebody was waving to us and a man dashed to our boat to drag it as far on shore as possible. He had horses and a cart waiting for us. Reloading was done very swiftly and soon we were on our way through a countryside which was quite new to me. We joined a stream of other carts and people on foot, as well as some cattle. Everyone looked frightened and every now and then kept glancing over their shoulders as if expecting some monster to be following us.

I was quite tired and very hungry by the time we reached a little town. We found a railway station on its outskirts, surrounded by crowds of people and by what to me, looked like mountains of furniture and household and farm gear as well as some cows - all waiting for the train. Little Olenka could not accept that one usually has to wait for the train. She raised such a loud protest that mother had no choice but satisfy her hunger and other needs, right there and then. The train was still not there. This encouraged Genio and myself to make it known that our tummies were also very unhappy. After a few futile attempts to hush us mother gave in and opened a large wicker basket where I could see all sorts of goodies. Without any delay we all got a piece of bread in one hand and a chunk of cheese in the other.

We were happily munching when we suddenly heard a commotion at the far end of the station. Somebody must have spotted the puffs of smoke of the approaching train. Mother hastily fastened the basket and I was gulping down the last mouthful when the train arrived. As it was slowing down we could clearly see that it consisted of a mixture of passenger and goods coaches. When it stopped the doors were flung open with a crash and a feverish loading began.

Where our heavier things went I don't know but we ourselves, with only our hand luggage, were directed into a passenger coach. Father, who regarded the gramophone as our prize possession, attempted to get in with the machine and its horn. Unfortunately the horn was too wide and got stuck in the door but only for a few seconds because some railway official or soldier snatched it out of father's hands and flung it over people's heads into the field. I could see outrage and murder on my father's face, but there was no question of arguing or trying to retrieve it - the mood of the crowd trying to embark was too explosive. After a lot of arranging and rearranging we settled down and a little later our train started moving.

Olenka was the only one who had received her full feed before we left and was soon fast asleep in mother's arms. Mother carefully passed her on to Ivdokya and pulled the precious basket nearer to herself. This time there were no interruptions to our meal.

By now it was quite dark outside. Sleeping in those conditions would normally be rather difficult, but with my tummy satisfied and the rhythmic swaying of the coach I found it quite impossible to keep my eyes open. When the train stopped with a jolt I woke to find my head on my mother's lap. There was a lot of peering through the windows and someone even opened the door trying to get a better view forward. Nothing was visible and one could hear the soporific sighing of the locomotive. We must have stopped and started many times during that night.

When I finally woke up it was getting light and we were approaching a bigger town. More and more houses could be seen and our progress became slower until we finally stopped at a bustling station. We were told to stay in the carriage. The adults were crowding at the windows making it impossible for me to see what was going on. Mother told us that we would have to wait here to change trains.

After a while we were shunted to an outside platform next to a long line of goods trucks. Father and Ivdokya jumped out and disappeared for quite a long time whilst mother sorted out our belongings. Eventually father returned and helped us all down. All our bits and pieces were deposited around us. Father pointed to one of the trucks and said something to mother to which she reacted with scorn. Nevertheless from now on we were to travel in one of the goods trucks. She took the baby and made us follow her to the truck door from which Ivdokya was extending her arms to take us up one by one. Next she jumped down and ran to father to help him to carry the luggage. Mother was mollified by the fact that we had the whole truck to ourselves.

This change suited me fine because by now the sun was high and we were getting warm. The door had to stay open but before we moved off three scouts arrived carrying their long sticks and explained that they had been sent to the trucks in which young children were travelling. Their task was to use their sticks to construct a kind of a barrier across the door to prevent us falling out.

Now our progress was even slower than before; we must have been given the lowest priority of all the rail traffic. On many occasions we were held up in a siding to let other trains go by in the opposite direction, carrying soldiers, trucks, guns and all sorts of gear. One of these trains had no lorries or guns but I could see lots and lots of horses. Occasionally I could hear the soldiers singing!

"They must be going to deal with that monster which frightened my parents" I thought to myself.

13

We had to stop so often and when we moved, we moved so slowly that people had time to get out not only for "calls of nature" but also to pick up any available vegetables, gather berries and look for water. This kind of progress lasted for six days and nights. Cooking, eating and sleeping had to take place on the train.

Our Primus stove proved its value many times over as it was "buzzing" for many hours a day. The scouts arranged a kind of tripod from which the kettle or a pan would be suspended whilst the Primus would be safely bedded in a layer of sand in a box. Thus neither would be upset by a sudden lurch of the wagon. Father had to jump out at some of the stops if there was any chance of doing some shopping. At one of these stops he managed to buy a chicken. Next my mother had to spend a lot of time preparing the bird then cooking it. This required frequent pumping of the Primus but in the end we had wonderful chicken soup with barley, onions and carrots. The bird itself had to be saved for the next day.

One morning our train stopped near a river and we were told that it would be several hours before we would get permission to proceed. Even the locomotive stopped its reassuring "chuff – chuff". One woman took the opportunity to carry her washing to the gravely bank. Following her example many more joined her and soon the whole length of the train reverberated to the noise of the rapid clapping of wooden bats beating the laundry against flat stones, mixed with their piercing voices exchanging gossip. Soon the various shapes and colours of the washing were flapping from lines stretched between the wagons or the nearest trees.

A few stops after that we reached our final stop where we were ordered to disembark. Thus in the early summer of 1920 we arrived at a place called Leszno, near the western border of reborn Poland, to begin our new life.

Poland's changing borders and neighbours (1939 with modern Poland superimposed)

Poland - Summer 1939

A messenger came to summon me to the Commanding Officer. The Adjutant simply nodded his head towards the chief's door indicating that I was expected. I knocked, entered and saluted. Captain Buczama was standing by the window with a sheet of paper in his hand. He acknowledged my salute and said

"Lieutenant, you are to report to the training unit in Warsaw where you will attend a short course in camouflage. Here are the details and train timetable; I am afraid it means leaving within the next two hours. I will speak to your Warrant Officer and ask him to deputise for you here. As you know he is a very experienced man."

"Yes Sir." I answered. "How long am I expected to be away?"

"It is supposed to be a week's course but since it started this morning you should be back on Saturday 26th. Goodbye Lieutenant and look out, the Warsaw girls like our new style uniform."

I smiled, saluted and going out, I saw my deputy already waiting in the adjutant's office. He must have been told what was in the air.

"Don't worry Sir, everything will be in order. See you next week."

He added a rather spicy remark about the girls in the capital city. We both laughed and shook hands. I had to hurry to put a few things together, have a meal and get myself to the station.

Upon arrival in the city I went to the hotel indicated on my posting papers where I found that I wasn't the only Air Force man hurriedly posted on this course. Two more lieutenants were already there, signing in and getting their room numbers.

We were told to attend an evening lecture at which we found mostly Army and Cavalry officers. The following day we were taken to the nearest "polygon" - a good-sized chunk of countryside set aside entirely for the purpose of military training. Our instructor conducted us to a group of pine and birch trees with very little other vegetation around. Next he spent a few minutes talking about the choice of materials and colours to suit our surroundings. Then we were invited to offer our ideas for hiding, for instance, a group of fully armed soldiers. Our suggestions were coming from all directions when he suddenly blew a whistle! We immediately stopped talking and to our great surprise noticed that the small sand hills and bushes started moving and revealing that we had been standing and rather light-heartedly discussing some aspects of effective camouflage right in the middle of a very cleverly hidden army platoon. Machine guns and personnel arms were all pointing at us, all covered by nets with bits of vegetation stuck here and there.

This particular demonstration impressed us tremendously and we were looking forward to a similar exercise; one which included transport and even aircraft. The next day was spent mostly on lectures. We were trying to listen to the lecturer but it was rather difficult as there was some kind of unease in the air, especially when one senior officer was signalled to leave the lecture room.

On Thursday, August 24th, after more lectures and a rather late lunch, we were assembling for another session of practical demonstration when the Officer in Charge came in and announced that the course had been suspended and that we were to return to our units within the next 24 hours. That sounded ominous.

Some of our group worked out that we could have time for a night on the town and still report to the units on time. I decided to take the first suburban train to Podkowa Lesna, a suburb of Warsaw, where my Auntie Anna lived with her daughter, Maryla and granddaughter, Krystyna. As I had expected to be in Warsaw for a whole week I had promised to pop in for a chat. They had been very kind to me during my final years at the Cadet School in Warsaw. This was not so long ago, only about six months earlier when my unit was transferred to...

...but, let's start at the beginning.

With my fellow air cadet students, c. 1939.

In September 1935, after my matriculation exams and a good holiday I was conscripted into the Army. There was no choice, even though my dreams for many years had been to join the Air Force and serve as a pilot! I had to put up with the infantry drills, parades, cleaning rifles every day and polishing boots every evening, inspections, marching, running and so on until...YES...UNTIL!

The most consequential thing of my life was when a notice appeared on the notice board in January 1936. It predestined my future and now, many years later, I am convinced that it also extended my life! Can you imagine anything more tremendous in one's life? The notice appealed for volunteers to apply for transfer to the Air Force Commissioning School for training to become Air Force Technical Officers of a squadron. This meant regular service - service for life. But being attached and working in a squadron would place me very near to flying! I couldn't get any nearer.

Two of us applied. A few days later we had to face interviews and were accepted. Apparently my school records in mathematics and science were impressive enough. The following week we were posted to a newly created military school in a town half way between Warsaw and Gdansk. It was in a cavalry barracks that had only recently been converted into classrooms, elementary laboratories, workshops, dormitories, etc. Our programme had only a few hours per week of drills and marching but every morning we had some vigorous exercises ending with a long run followed by a nice hot shower.

A year later we were transferred to Warsaw into purpose-built and much larger premises fully equipped for residence, lecture rooms, laboratories as required for studies in Mechanical Engineering Science and Aerodynamics at University level. There was enough room to accommodate two more annual intakes of about 30 cadets a year. All of this was next door to an airfield with the sights and sounds of aircraft. This pleasure was magnified for me by the fact that my Auntie Anna and her family were not far away.

So...back to 1939 and my curtailed course. My visit to Aunt Anna's family was very brief; we literally had only a few minutes for greetings, hugs and kisses before we had to dash to the station. Jumping onto the train I shouted: "See you soon!" Little did I know that I would not see them or any of my family for 21 years!

It was quite obvious that these sudden orders meant only one thing – the political situation was rapidly deteriorating. Hitler was demanding more and more of "Lebensraum" and the threat of war that hung over our heads for the last few months changed from a threat to an imminent danger.

My family in Leszno, c.1939 – from left to right: Me, my brother Genio, my Mother, my sister Olenka, my Father

From my previous years in Warsaw I knew that I had time to catch a train going west with connection for Leszno where I could have just a few hours with my family before proceeding on to Krakow. My arrival at home was completely unexpected and rather late in the night - but what parents mind that? Especially when in their hearts they knew that it may be months or even years before my next visit. My parents, together with my sister Olga (a diminutive form of Olenka as used by my family), were very emotional about it all, whilst my own mind did not seem to accept the full meaning of what was happening…or what was about to happen.

In the morning I found my girlfriend, Victoria, who took me for a walk through the main square under the pretext of some urgent shopping for her mother. I suspected that all she wanted was to impress her friends with her young man in the brand new uniform of a Second Lieutenant in the Air Force. I was equally proud of her because she was the most beautiful girl in town to my eyes, with her long gold-blonde hair and blue eyes.

Our new uniforms were quite distinct from the rest of the Armed Forces seen in this town, which was a garrison for an Army and Cavalry regiment. The nearest Air Force Station was about 50 miles away and the sea was about 300 miles north, thus one rarely saw a blue uniform in Leszno. We wore light blue and our hats were round, as opposed to the general khaki and square hats. But the biggest attraction and the envy of young boys was our sidearm, a foot-long dagger with a white ivory handle.

Much too soon came the time to say good-bye to them all, except my brother Genio, who was already away with his army unit. A fast train got me back to my Squadron "within 24 hours". The aerodrome was buzzing with activity and my squadron was already half loaded on its transport. This annoyed me slightly because I felt I should have been recalled sooner or, in my opinion, not sent out at all. To make matters worse my C.O. told me that according to the mobilisation plans I was to transfer to a completely new unit called the Mobile Repair Unit No 2 (known as P.R.2, which in English would be M.W.2 or Mobile Workshop No. 2).

This really upset me because I had to leave all my friends and undertake the organisation of a thus far non-existent Unit. I begged my ex-C.O. to at least allow me to complete the preparations for the squadron's departure. He agreed with alacrity as he was already behind schedule and the new Technical Officer to the Squadron, my replacement, had only just arrived from reserves and needed a few days to pick up the routine.

By Saturday evening the ground crew and everything that goes with keeping a squadron of fighter aircraft in the air was ready and they left for a destination simply described as –"the field". A couple of hours earlier I had watched the aircraft taking off in groups of three and heading in a north-easterly direction.

My next 24 hours were spent studying the organisation of the new Unit. I had to read and re-read many lists and instructions - one had to know everything almost by heart. A few N.C.O.s (non-commissioned Officers) and airmen had already been transferred from the Squadron to P.R.2. Our first task was to collect the lorries allocated to us and then set about drawing the equipment and materials for our workshop to thus create the main part of the P.R.2. On Wednesday morning reservists started arriving straight from "civvy street" and my duty was to stay in the reception room and select all those whose trade or training made them qualified for a repair workshop. By the end of the day I must have interviewed about 100 men and managed to find only 72 suitable for our kind of job. Whilst I was thus occupied, a very good friend of mine, Dominik appeared and informed that he had also been posted to the P.R.2.

The N.C.O.s organised transfer of materials to the hangar allocated to our Unit. Now all that remained to do was to enlist a few more men and then to go shopping for fresh food. I must add that there were not enough uniforms to go round, so some had civilian trousers with a blue battle-dress top or vice versa. The blue uniforms for the air force had been only recently introduced and the production rate was only geared to peacetime.

By late evening on Thursday we were too tired to carry on any longer; Dominik and I simply dropped onto our beds. Henry, who shared the room with us, was already fast asleep. His function was the anti-aircraft defence of the base. The base was a couple of miles in diameter containing the airfield, aircraft, hangars, command buildings, officers and men's quarters housing at least 1000 men. Henry had only one Oerlikon gun capable of zenithal fire, plus a few machine guns placed round the perimeter of the aerodrome. I am quoting all this detail to show the actual state of Poland's 'warlike aggressive stance' as alleged by Hitler.

I remember Henry mentioning that he was responsible for receiving a load of bombs for our bombers. Very wisely he had them stacked at the far end of the airfield, a long way away from everybody and everything. His powerful motorbike, a Norton, came in very useful since Henry quite often had to chase from one end of the base to the other. While drifting off to sleep I felt that we could report our Unit ready for further orders.

I awoke suddenly, shaken by violent explosions. I looked at my watch; it was 5:23 am. So, as I jumped out of bed I shouted to Henry: "Your bombs must be going off! We've got saboteurs! Fifth column!" We dashed to the window and there we saw our "saboteurs" in the form of German Dorniers flying very low and dropping bombs wherever they pleased.

THIS IS IT!!   WAR!!!

The long expected struggle had begun. All those negotiations and appeasements had come to nothing, as many of us in our hearts had long known they would. The engine roar and bomb blasts abated but as I looked out of the window I saw a solitary Stuka dive-bomber screaming down onto the wing of the Command building where the office with all the mobilisation plans and documents were located. How was that for "fifth column" expertise in gathering information? Almost simultaneously a bomb struck the far end of our Officers' block. It did not seem to bother us. I suppose the danger of it all had not really sunk in.

I dressed quickly and put on my leather coat and beret. Picking up my gas mask, I went out towards the men's quarters. I was not on my own; some others had the same idea. A few hundred steps further on we were stopped by Colonel Kuzmierski. He advised us to drop into the nearest trench whilst the raid lasted. The wise old fox knew that such violent raids cannot be sustained for long and that the lives of young officers, however inexperienced, brave and foolish, were valuable.

The next stick of bombs made a proper mess of the Officers' block. Roof tiles and bricks were flying in all directions and all we could do was to crouch in a very inadequate shallow trench and wait for the flying debris to settle down without depositing anything heavy on our heads. I kept my head down and waited for the thumps and crashes around us to die down. When we looked out we saw smoke billowing from some of the hangars and a generally frightful mess all around us.

Suddenly we were conscious of a peculiar smell. It was enough for someone to shout: "Gas"! - more as a question than a statement and our gas masks were on our faces faster than in any training session. The Gas Officer would have been pleased. We felt a little stupid when we saw some men shuffling along aimlessly completely dazed but without any obvious effects of gas. It transpired that the suspicious smell was due to a combination of smoke and morning mist together with a burst gas main nearby. We didn't wait any longer. Besides, the raiders seemed satisfied with their bloody work and there was now much less aircraft noise.

Instead, we could hear the crackling of fires and the lamentations and moans of the wounded and dying. Two of us ran in the direction of our men's lodgings. Near the first hut a headless body gave us a shock but it prepared us for worse things to come. My Unit was housed a bit further on. Men were already jumping out from the trenches and whatever other hiding places they had found. By the well I saw a soldier moaning and staggering about with his hands across his stomach and with his entrails dragging behind. "Oh Lord! I cannot stop to help him!" Even if I did I couldn't help him except by shortening his agony with a bullet from my pistol. My men were now my priority. They were already assembling with surprising calmness and orderliness.

The raid now over, we marched to our hangar to assess the damage and losses. Not as much as we had feared. The roof was in bad shape, a few holes in the lorries and a few windscreens smashed. I knew that our emergency dispersal point was only about 10 miles from Krakow, so we began immediate preparations to evacuate lock, stock and barrel as fast as we could before the next raid. As soon as a lorry was loaded it was sent on its way to unload and come back for more. It required two journeys by each vehicle to move all the equipment and men.

I sent my senior N.C.O. and my driver on the motorcycle to look after the other end. Effective camouflage was their priority. They had to be in readiness for repair work and, rather importantly, prepare a meal for us all.   As to the air-raid defence of our new position in the positive sense - no priority at all! Why? Because in spite of my persistent demands we were not issued with even one machine gun and we only had forty rifles for the proposed full strength of over 80 men.   The answer to my demands was:

"Wiser and more experienced people decided about it and we haven't enough arms anyway".

Weighing it up now, after the event, I feel that even ten machine guns would not have made much difference to the history of our Unit. Besides, our object was not to attack but to keep our aircraft in good repair and good flying order for those who were trained to attack.

The last pieces of equipment and stores were on their way.   My driver came back for me on the motorcycle, so I put on my goggles and settled in the sidecar to follow the last lorry.   A few miles out we found one of our lorries (a Bulldog) partly in a ditch and burnt out. Apparently it was the victim of a single raider who pounced on it and killed the only Warrant Officer I had.   This was an irreparable loss - with him was also a corporal, one of our experienced drivers.   At the dispersal point I found a lot of activity.   There I was given the news that the lieutenant appointed as our C.O. had been driven by Dominik to make contact with the fighter squadrons that we were to support and keep in repair.

Lorries and stacks of stores were hidden under trees and the men were given their well-earned meal; thick pea soup with chunks of smoked bacon floating in it and plenty of bread. Was it good?! - only then did I realise that I had had no breakfast that day. After the meal I asked for a detailed report of our losses and issued orders for the night watch.   It transpired that apart from the W.O. and corporal driver we had lost another N.C.O. and two men in the first day of the war. At this rate we wouldn't last long! With these grim thoughts I went to the farmhouse that my quartermaster had secured for some of us.

At about 22.00hrs when it was quite dark, I decided to check the vigilance of our sentries. After all, most of them had only been carpenters, locksmiths, clerks, etc a few days before and now they were fighting a war. I came out of the building and for a good minute could not see a single thing, not even the outline of the lorries or trees. There was no moon and not a single light anywhere. Gradually I could discern the black outline of trees against the dark velvet sky. Under those trees were our lorries. As quietly as I could I moved in that direction but before I could get anywhere near them a voice called out of the blackness:

"Stop! Who goes there?"

I could just dimly see a long shiny object pointing at me and I heard the ominous click of the safety catch on the rifle. Oh! This is for real! I froze and quietly replied "Friend". I was frightened that I could be facing a jittery young reservist with a head full of facts and fiction about the "fifth column". He asked the question "Parole?" to which I gave him the required answer and in turn asked for the predetermined response. This pacified the sentry and he allowed me to come nearer but I noticed that he still held the rifle in a position of readiness. This was the result of good training as much as fear of the dreaded "fifth column". After a few words about nothing in particular he visibly relaxed and admitted that only then was he certain of who he was challenging. He recognised my voice. This exchange must have been overheard by other sentries in the still night, for I had no difficulty in completing the round. Then back to my quarters and to bed.

With sunrise the camp came to life expecting a repeat

performance of yesterday's bombing and we were not disappointed. The Dorniers and Stukas were back but our position remained undiscovered. Nobody was allowed to move outside the tree line. No telltale footpaths were created criss-crossing the fields and the little village appeared as peaceful as usual.

After the raiders left, new columns of smoke rising from our hapless aerodrome were visible even from this distance. We had our breakfast and put the watch in position. Dominik arrived with new orders for our Unit. We were to embark onto a train at a sub-station in Krakow and proceed to Lodz, about 120 miles to the north. The train would be ready for us by noon.

The first lorries left at mid-morning and arrived at the loading point to the accompaniment of the roar of aircraft and the thunder of bombs. The loading of the train took until late afternoon but we achieved this without incident and were ready and eager to move off so as to arrive at Lodz before daybreak. No such luck! We spent most of the night immobilised for some obscure reason and did not leave until about 4.00am. On our way we had frequent sightings of single or more raiders attacking non-too-distant targets. Lookouts had been stationed on the roofs of the wagons. I had ordered that as soon as they signalled a sighting of a raid near to us the train had to come to a halt and everybody had to jump off and scatter in all directions in the fields. This would at least reduce, if not prevent, casualties due to aircraft machine guns or bombs. This was not too difficult as the train was merely crawling along.

After a couple of hours of this laborious progress we reached a station which had just been bombed. There was some damage to the rails but the repair crew assured us of only an hour or two's delay so our cooks got busy! Also, to restore the sagging spirits caused by our frequent running away from the train, the N.C.O.s sent all those who possessed rifles to hide under a line of trees on a ridge overlooking the station. They also had to be given instructions as to how to aim at flying aircraft. We realised that there was only a minute chance of hitting one but at least they would not be running. I could almost hear them wishing for one damn Dornier to appear. There really would be an enthusiastic and tremendous fusillade…and such a waste of ammo!

Repairs took longer than estimated by the enthusiastic repair team and so it was late afternoon before we started again. At dusk our train was only moving at walking pace and eventually stopped. When I remonstrated with the driver he bluntly told me that his orders were not to move unless he was certain about the state of the line ahead. He was to avoid derailment at all costs. The sense of it was obvious so we had to suffer another uncomfortable night. At dusk we began our crawl again and reached a town which, to our surprise, was not badly damaged. We did not want to press our luck and moved on towards our destination.

Unfortunately only a few miles further on we were stopped by more bomb damage and another air raid. This time it was of a quite different nature because the aircraft kept at a good height. I was quite intrigued by their tactic until I heard a frequent "pom!! pom!!" sound coming from the nearby woods. Of course!…an anti-aircraft gun! The first on our route! The 'brave' bombers did not dare to come down below about 3,000 metres - one solitary anti-aircraft gun keeping them up there. A beautiful little Oerlikon (that was its name, I think) was sending shells right under the Dorniers bellies. Quite a few of us gathered behind the gunners and we could see the shells zooming up and almost touching the damned bombers but at the same time reaching the apex of their trajectory and gently curving their path to fly under the raiders and finally begin their descent. The sight of this made us groan with fury!!

"A few metres higher!!" - as if our yelling could improve things.

After the raid it transpired that we had stopped in an almighty hot spot. The track ran through woods that concealed a great mass of military depots. Hence the anti-aircraft gun. Obviously, it would have been unwise to add a train-load of men and equipment as further bait for the Luftwaffe's appetite. So we started building a ramp from ripped up rail sleepers, earth, rock and anything else useful to hand. We were very fortunate to have a rail hut with some repair tools that proved just as useful for a dismantling job. Then, by shunting the train a little at a time, we had all the vehicles off. There were many hair-raising moments but once again I thanked the Almighty for our skilful drivers. In two trips the men and equipment were safely shifted into the woods behind a village a few miles down the road.

During our overnight stop I decided to call a kind of conference with the N.C.O.s. It did not take much explaining that our situation was becoming more and more hopeless. News picked up from people fleeing south-east from Warsaw was frightful. The City was suffering a merciless demolition by both air raids and tanks! These must have come from East Prussia.

With all this in my mind, together with the complete lack of contact with our squadrons I recommended the following priorities:

1. Safety, health and good spirit of all and of our drivers in particular.
2. Perfect maintenance of lorries and economy of petrol.
3. Constant lookout for enemy aircraft.
4. Have our eyes open to spot potential "fifth column" agents.

We finished by praying for some inspiration as how to save lives and, if at all possible, avoid capture by the enemy.

The next day was the day for discarding everything that was not indispensable. From now on we had to become more mobile and reduce the double journeys as, at our present rate of progress, petrol would soon become a problem. The fuel reserves were distributed so that each lorry had its own barrel, making it safer and giving the drivers a more equal chance. They were also encouraged to fill up wherever and whenever they could before dipping into the reserves. Here and there were abandoned or damaged cars, still with some petrol in their tanks, giving us the opportunity to siphon out a few litres.

Although everything was ready by the evening I found that almost everyone was exhausted, so we stayed the night. A cottager offered me a bed. I tried to sleep but with so many problems whirling in my head I found it quite impossible. The main problem was the complete lack of information or further instructions. Should I press on to the city of Lodz? Should I send only a messenger on my motorcycle to reconnoitre and locate the nearest military centre where he could find out the whereabouts of Squadrons 122 and 123?

I had had no contact with the H.Q. for many days. My C.O. and Dominik had left Krakow by car promising to rejoin me in Lodz. With all that going round in my head I got out of bed and went outside hoping the cool night would calm me down. Instead, I was astounded by the scene around me. A semicircle of fires along the western horizon with sporadic flashes followed by the deep roar of guns. Hardly anybody had much sleep that night. I do not know how long I had slept when I was woken by one of the sergeants soon after dawn. Most of the men were already out and watching the smoky horizon, illuminated by flashes here and there. Anxiety was written all over their faces. We then saw a few, a very few, pieces of our field artillery retreating further east, beyond our position. A number of soldiers went by; most of them were wounded. This was all the more alarming, so I asked one of them to give me some idea of the situation. He pointed to the smoking horizon and said: "The front was there last night!"

It did not take us long after that to have the first group of vehicles moving with instructions to aim for our next assembly point. Quite obviously no air force squadrons would be stationed so near to the front and consequently no support group would be expected in this area. The German advance must have been really swift. They had covered 80 miles in four days and so resistance could not have been very effective. The sensible thing for us now was to change direction for Warsaw.

I wanted to make sure that the first group of vehicles was not bunched up, so giving the Luftwaffe an easy target, and that all were moving on the agreed route. So I followed the first group in the sidecar of my motorbike with Corporal Zurski at the controls. The road surface was quite good and there was not too much vehicular traffic. Some soldiers and very many civilians were all walking in the same direction but the noise of our motorbike made sure that we had a pretty easy passage. We soon caught up with the head of our stretched out column and outside a little town I asked my driver to stop. After a brief chat with the N.C.O. in charge of the leading lorry we left them to carry on and turned back towards our starting point to check on the progress of the second column.

Just then the thunder of bombs drew our eyes to a formation of Dorniers flying over the road and bombing and machine-gunning anything that moved. They continued in this fashion right over the town we had just left. Their north-easterly course took them away from us since we had now deviated in a more easterly direction. My worry was that the rest of our vehicles were somewhere between the woods and the little town. The picture of the smouldering remnants of our "Bulldog", when we were still near Krakow, flashed into my mind. I called our "doctor", the first aid man, to hop on the pillion and come with me. Hrumyk, one of my most experienced N.C.O.s was in that group and I just could not bear the thought of losing this man after the loss of the W.O. on the first day. We rattled into the town where we now found many more frightened and confused people on the road. A corner house was burning, laying a thick cloud of smoke and tongues of flame across the road. A little further on a small building had literally been blown to pieces, together with a group of soldiers who had the misfortune to be hiding under its eaves. Corporal Zurski was too busy avoiding people who were wandering about aimlessly to notice we had run over a rifle with a forearm still holding it. On our return trip I learned that these unfortunate victims were three young army cadets.

The stretch of road, which looked to us to have been so violently bombed, did not have too many craters. The majority were scattered in the fields on either side. Was this done on purpose? To terrorise the population into confusion and flight but at the same time to leave the roads in a sufficiently good state to ensure a quick progress of their own motorised units?

Near the edge of the woods we met the remaining lorries. Most men were still quite obviously shocked but the wonderful drivers had tried to carry on as if nothing had happened. Sgt Hrumyk told me that as soon as his lookouts reported bombers approaching he stopped the vehicles and signalled for all to scatter. When he got back to his lorry he found a crater not many feet in front of it and the windscreen shattered – a delay of only a couple of seconds would have been fatal.

It did not take us long to get organised and moving on to the assembly point. There we had to leave part of the load under guard once again - in the charge of a sergeant who had been a teacher only six days previously.

The next stop was to be just beyond a town called Radom. I remained with them for a while allowing the first lot to put a few miles between us. My role was similar to that of a sheepdog; racing ahead to see that the head of the column was safe and then tearing back to make sure that there were no unpleasant incidents at the tail end. This continuous travelling in an open sidecar in clouds of dust deposited a layer of powder on my goggles. At a hold-up I took them off to blow them to clean the dust off. The rubbery frames of the glass were covered with a heavy layer. Wiping my cheeks I collected a lump of a sticky mixture of sweat and dust. I did not bother to look in the driver's mirror!

After a while we somehow managed to overtake the slow moving crowd and found the road much easier. With the increased speed we rolled happily along when to our horror we saw soil and turnips flying into the air only a few hundred yards in front of us!

"Damn the bastards!! STOP!!"

Off the motorbike and off the road into a field which, to our dismay, had no trees or bushes to hide under or at least to make us less conspicuous. I was not so much concerned about the bombs as about the vicious machine-gunners who could direct their fire to either side of their flight path. The roar of the engines was directly overhead; the aircraft was not more than 1000 feet above us. This was the moment of utmost danger. I could almost feel the malicious eyes of some Nazi bomb-aimer or gunner on my head estimating the best point for dropping a bomb or opening fire. The familiar whistle of falling bombs penetrated the engine roar. I flattened myself into a shallow trench between rows of turnips and from the corner of my eye could see my driver doing exactly the same. Almost simultaneously shrapnel bombs could be heard exploding above us. The bloody swine was throwing antipersonnel bombs! Fragments of metal were splattering around us and I felt a helplessly vulnerable target. Talk about sitting ducks! - except that we were prostrated and perfectly visible. Wondering whether my leather jacket presented any kind of barrier to flying metal, I tensed myself expecting to hear the rear-gunners fire. Nothing happened! Phew! – air raid over: back to the motorbike and off again.

From now on it was my job to keep a sharp lookout forward and backward for more raiders. Towards the evening we found our forward column comfortably established in a small clearing. Two Fiats with Corporal Piotrowski in charge were despatched to fetch the rest of the materials and men whilst a meal was prepared. The quartermaster had found a barn to accommodate most of the men and quite a few of them had made themselves so comfortable on the lorries and in the workshop trucks that they would have preferred to stay there. He also told me that he had seen what looked like a large house a little further away. We set off immediately and after quarter of an hour of stumbling over quite rough ground we came within sight of a country mansion with a park and gardens of quite imposing proportions.

We wondered what kind of reception we would get but we were in for a pleasant surprise. A housemaid answered the doorbell and she took us into the drawing room where a lady and her two daughters were sitting. We clicked our heels and bowed as smartly as we could and I introduced the sergeant and myself. The ladies looked at us with big eyes in which I could see a mixture of fear and mirth. We must have looked both terrible and terrifying. This lasted but for a moment and the lady got up, smiled and extended her hand. In our gallant Polish fashion we kissed it. Our hostess said we were welcome to a meal but first:

"Would you like a bath?"

Of all the...!! But then it dawned on me that neither of us had a bath for a week. The weather was warm for September, the roads were dusty and a lot of it had settled on us in thick layers. We gladly accepted the suggestion and since this mansion had at least two bathrooms we were soon splashing happily. I washed my hair to complete the luxury.

Half an hour later we were enjoying our first civilised meal for a week; a cloth on the table, napkins and a maid serving a modest but very tasty repast. With some effort we restrained ourselves from wolfing it all before the ladies had even started. The daughters soon got used to our intrusion - after all, the new Air Force uniforms were supposed to perform miracles. Mother was getting more and more protective but she needn't have worried - we had to be back with our men.

The frequency of day raids made me decide that we could only travel by night from now on. Soon after midnight the men were roused from their short sleep. I explained the new method of progress and promised a good day's rest and by 2.00am all the vehicles were on their way. Corporal Piotrowski was expected to catch up with us well before midnight. So, with my driver and Lance Corporal Bras, we remained there until 3.00am but still we did not see them coming. Only a few horse-drawn carts with their half-asleep drivers and huddled dark figures swaying about sideways and backwards and forwards with each bump on the road. We could not wait any longer and so went on to the appointed place expecting to find the first part of the convoy. No sign of any vehicles and no men!! After a brief investigation of one or two possibilities without result I had the very unpleasant vision of becoming the leader of a non-existent convoy of lorries.

The light grey veil of the dawn was spreading higher and higher. The view of the nearby countryside became clearly visible and with it the horrible devastation of two villages which stretched along a street parallel to the main road. The weird sight of fireplaces and chimneys standing like tombstones, with morning mist and wisps of smoke gently swirling around them. They looked like ghosts and made my skin creep. This was all that remained of cottages built of wood and thatch. They must have burned fiercely leaving only the incombustible stone to stand like gravestones in memory of innocent peasants who had either died there or fled in terror. Thus depressed, we sped on towards Pulawy and there we saw our own lorries coming towards us. The explanation offered was that they could not find any suitable hiding place near the agreed point but I wondered if there had been a little break down of discipline?

Six days of constant moving without any visible objective and with more and more snippets of information and rumours from the civilian population about the alarming advance of German armies from north, west and south (ie: from Prussia, Germany and Czechoslovakia) had had its effects. Besides, one could not discount the possibility of some "folksdeutsche" men in our unit. These people claimed they were of German origin and that they were coerced to join the Polish armed forces and their dearest desire was to desert and to join the German army. Some of them might have been issued with rifles and so a small group could give us a lot of trouble. About a month later my suspicions were confirmed. It worried me immensely but I had no one to discuss it with and I dared not admit to anyone what I felt.

We were not far from Pulawy and the bridge over the Vistula so I decided to risk a couple of hours of daylight driving. Once again we had to start pushing our way through the crowds of pedestrians and carts streaming east. We found the bridge in a shaky but passable condition. There were holes in the road surface but no serious damage to the main structure so we held our breath and gingerly crossed over into Eastern Poland. As soon as we could, we turned north into promising looking, high pine woods which came right down to the riverbank. Before we settled down we had a grandstand view of the Luftwaffe attempting to destroy the bridge. There was some anti-aircraft defence so the planes flew high and in consequence there was a lot of noise and tons of water and mud thrown sky-wards but the bridge was still there when everything had calmed down. Very soon afterwards we could see the tiny silhouettes of people, carts and occasional cars crossing over…but much more slowly this time. To give the men a well-deserved rest I decided to stop there for two days.

I was still hoping that the lost corporal and the two vehicles would be seen crossing the bridge. In the meantime, somebody discovered two barges tied up under a line of overhanging trees. With great hopes of finding some good food we went to investigate. To our disgust both contained nothing but tons of sugar! Our own supplies were going down but were far from exhausted so, together with some fresh vegetables and fruit bought or "found", we had good meals that day.

We felt much safer and more relaxed being on the other side of our great river. Towards dusk the lookouts were posted and everybody clse was encouraged to get a good night's rest. The woods consisted mainly of high pine trees standing in a year's thick carpet of pine needles. The lowest branches formed a huge umbrella about three feet above the ground. I crawled under to explore one such tree with a view of converting it into my bedroom. I found it to be very cosy. After a good meal and chat with my N.C.O.s I bid them all "goodnight" and crept into my luxury flat. It was wonderful! Soft, warm, peaceful and full of the aroma of pine tree resin. I had one of my best night's sleep there.

We were only a dozen or so miles from the well known Air Force Flying School in Deblin so after breakfast I explained to Sgt Hrumyk about my plan to visit Deblin H.Q. with a view to obtain reliable information and possibly some instructions for our unit. "You are in charge here now. Let the men relax all day but they must not leave our perimeter without your permission for more than an hour. Keep a sharp look out for Corp. Piotrowski." I added, scrambling into the sidecar.

The ride along the river bank would have been my idea of a holiday were it not for the heavy stream of lorries, cars, carts and the mass of walking humanity...all going in the opposite direction! I did not like it at all! When we finally arrived at the airfield we found the H.Q. buildings in varying degrees of disintegration. Some were still burning and there were a few aircraft with wings or tails at incongruous angles to the fuselage. The field was dotted with bomb craters. We were about to make a U-turn when I saw a figure emerging from one of the half-ruined buildings. We rode up to him and I shuddered at the sight of a pair of fatigued eyes full of hopelessness and defeat. His answers to my questions were very brief:

"Warsaw under incessant bombardment. The Government... with all its gear...moving south-east. This aerodrome was evacuated a few days ago and I will follow them as soon as I can; that is, as soon as I have burned what is left of the important documents in these ruins. In two days time I hope to be in Lwow".

This was almost too much for me. I was expecting some evidence of organised resistance being directed from this highly esteemed centre of training for the cream of the Polish Air Force: all I found was despair and devastation. I felt near tears when I remembered my last visit to this place.

I was in the third year at the Engineering College and in the curriculum was a flying course in light aircraft. Its purpose was to make us more aware of a pilot's difficulties and to note his remarks about the machine's airworthiness. At the end of the course we had to perform a solo flight cross-country to a selected aerodrome. It was a test of confidence and in navigation after which one was deemed qualified. The chosen aerodrome was of course Deblin. I remember approaching to land amongst at least half a dozen other machines landing or taking off. There were no runways in those days so you just slotted in between two others and 'Hey Presto!' I felt immensely proud to be amongst the elite of Polish pilots albeit in training. I had always envied them as my strongest desire was to be a pilot but my eyesight was not up to the high standard required at that stage. So I chose the second best and trained as an aircraft-engineering officer. If could not fly, I reasoned, at least I could be nearby and help those who could. After reporting to the flight office I was directed to the Cadet's Mess for refreshments since it was almost time for lunch.

There I could see puzzled looks on their faces mingled with an air of superiority as they tried to work out "What has this "plumber" got to do with flying?!" They obviously recognised my Engineers badge. Just the same I had a feeling of achievement being amongst the "Eaglets" after a solo flight from Warsaw. Many of them had not reached that stage yet in their training. But...this was not the time or place for reminiscence.

The twelve-mile return journey proved much slower and more difficult than expected. We reached our camp soon after noon and found the men in a state of agitation. Sergeant Hrumyk quickly reported that three men had declared themselves to be "folksdeutsche" and wanted to leave the unit. The rest were so angry that the sergeant had the utmost difficulty in preventing impromptu executions. I ordered that they should be treated as prisoners of war as we had no evidence of treason. They were to be placed under guard until we could hand them over to the Military Police.

Without any doubt the war was going badly for us. No contact with any Air Force authorities, the loss of two vehicles and some men, less and less petrol and, on top of all that, three prisoners to guard. How many more were there waiting to show their true colours...and how many of them were armed?

By the end of the day everybody must have heard about what we had found at Deblin and were ready to go. From now on we were only going to carry the absolute essentials so that there would be no need to send anybody back for the remaining equipment and men. Arrangements were made, the column formed and we set off towards Lwow.

Next morning found us in a village near a convent that was a shelter for orphans. We tried to have a day of rest but there was no peace, as we had to witness the bombing of a nearby airfield. The next night's travel brought us much nearer to Lwow. After a few hours rest in an orchard we moved closer still, to a small village where we spent the rest of the night. The following day it became quite obvious that in our ignorance of the situation, we had been much too optimistic. In our heads was some vague idea of the defence of Lwow as conjured by a historical fact well known to us. Some twenty years earlier the young people of Lwow ("young eagles" as they became known) had attempted a spirited if vain defence of the city against the Bolshevik invaders. It was thoughts of this fighting spirit that we all shared.

I took an N.C.O. with us and we drove by motorbike into the city hoping to make contact with the military authorities. The further we drove into the city the quieter the streets became. We were stopped by an officer in charge of two anti-tank guns placed either side of the street, their muzzles peering round the corners of buildings as if sniffing the air and expecting the stench of the diesel fumes from German tanks to excite them into action at any minute. The officer advised us to turn back and drive as fast as we could. German foot patrols were in the next block and their Panzer division was expected at any time. He gave me an address where I could get better information, with a bit of luck.

When we got there we found an army officer who was almost in despair with a transport problem. He was responsible for a group of yet unarmed reservists and had been promised army trucks to evacuate them from the town. I offered to help by taking his troop as far as the village where my column was encamped if they would meet our lorry at 19.00 hours by the old city gate. In the meantime artillery shells started falling nearer and nearer with fires breaking out in some of the buildings, so we made a quick dash to our group where we found everybody raring to go. Bad news had travelled faster than our motorbike; there was no point hiding the truth from them all. I emphasised to my N.C.O.s once again that from now on only the safety of the men mattered.

To avoid encirclement by the fast moving Panzer units we had to move east faster than the German tanks. For this reason the lorries were to carry only men, petrol and minimal personal luggage. There was enough room for all that and should one vehicle break down, we would be uncomfortable but still mobile. However, should we lose two vehicles....? I did not want to think about that just then. It made more sense to keep back just the two lorries selected for our possible rescue mission of the reservists and send the rest ahead to the next stopping place. Thus all but these two lorries were loaded and sent off and the remaining men had to be persuaded to stay put and await our return to pick them up.

Our meeting point was the old city gates and we arrived with at least half an hour to spare. The thunder of guns and mortars was increasing and we were extremely nervous but we had to stick it out. 19.00hrs came and went and no sign of the party of reservists. By 20.00hrs the rush of humanity rapidly decreased and a rather ominous silence punctuated by sporadic "boom-boom" started spreading its wings over the city. Either the reservist group could not make it or, let us hope, their own transport had arrived in time. We could not wait any longer and the drivers did not need any encouragement. We were off, stopping only to pick up the men who vacated the rescue mission lorries. It was obvious that they had had more than enough; a little longer and Sgt Hrumyk would have had a real revolt on his hands. I never ceased to admire the determination and professionalism of our N.C.O.s as well as the skill and endurance of the drivers.

Very soon we caught up with the slow-moving column of refugees and once again spent a few hours slowly overtaking the jostle of peasant wagons and over-loaded carts with white faces wobbling above them all. When we reached the next town we could not find the rest of our transport. They were expected to leave a lookout at the first building on our route to give us directions...there was nobody there. We were too tired by then, so we simply installed ourselves in a school for the rest of the night.

On the morning of September 13th our efforts to join the rest resulted in our being spotted by an Air Force Colonel who immediately took us under his command. His orders were: the men to be put on the train to Kolomyja while the lorries and a few men to proceed to the nearby aerodrome, where we were to fill up with petrol and to collect as many extra barrels of this precious liquid as we could find and deliver them to the Base 5 Command at Kolomyja.

This did not suit me at all because it meant delay and another separation from the rest. Besides – I had quite got used to being under nobody's orders and just pressing on further and further Southeast. But...."orders are orders", so I selected half a dozen men, quickly scanned the horizon and set off for the airfield.

Its appearance was similar to all the other airfields we had seen on our way. Buildings in various states of disrepair, no glass in any windows, the smell of burning everywhere and the smouldering remnants of aircraft. Suddenly, as if from underground, Major Peterek appeared and with an air of chagrin and exasperation pointed to the far end of the airfield saying:

"There are seven undamaged machines over there. They must be flown out towards Romania!"

I have to admit that at this moment I was sorely tempted to have my first and only wartime flight. The choice was not mine however, and so I allowed any volunteer with the required qualification to leave the Unit in order to save the aircraft. Only one, Leon, had a powered machine certificate - two others had some glider experience and were keen to take their chance. In my opinion it would have been foolish and we would have risked losing not only the aircraft but also the men. It would have been like allowing someone who had learned how to control a push-bike to ride a powerful motorbike, not on a little practice run but on a serious mission.

Anyway...first things first. There were some barrels with petrol in the bomb craters, which must have been considered the safest places to hide them according to the law that states "lightning doesn't strike the same place twice". They were too heavy to lift so we had to use a hand-pump to transfer the petrol to barrels on the lorries. This process took too much time for comfort. The men worked feverishly, always keeping an eye on the sky and ready to dive for cover. The fellow with the flying experience decided to take one aircraft out. We wished him luck and watched him run to the machines whilst we started driving out with about 3,000 litres of petrol.

We decided to stop for some food as we were passing through a little town. The sirens started at once and almost simultaneously we heard bombs thundering in the distance. This must have been at the airfield we had just left. All our thoughts went spontaneously to Leon, the volunteer, fervently wishing him to safety, miles away from here and still in the air. Concluding that the raiders were far too busy destroying what was left of the aerodrome we did not hurry. A bakery provided fresh bread and a farmer was glad to sell eggs, butter and fruit and we had a much-enjoyed snack a little further out.

By sheer luck we found Base 5 Command towards the evening. They were so "grateful" for our providing them with petrol that they promptly commandeered all the lorries and men! So now I was just an odd junior officer (only a Sub-Lieutenant) with nothing and nobody in particular to look after. No men or lorries to worry about, not even having to decide my next move because from now on I was receiving (!) orders. I was graciously permitted one final function; to see that my little band of men received a mug of hot milk in the village and were then found somewhere to sleep.

The place was literally swamped with men in uniform, so that late arrivals such as ourselves had to be satisfied with whatever was left. The lucky ones were on lorries, others under the trees and the ingenious ones on top of bushes. How could one do that you may ask? A blanket thrown over a strong, well-developed bush with a piece of string or a belt, to hold the bush together, could become quite a comfortable bed. The art was in getting on top and staying there until it bent to its angle of permanent inclination. My marvellous leather coat served as a cover not so much from cold as from the fine rain, which put an end to a long spell of fine weather. Too fine in fact - flying conditions were perfect....but only for German aircraft! I wistfully remembered the wonderful, dry, peaceful accommodation under the tall pine trees near Pulawy. That was like a three-star hotel by comparison.

In the morning, after a mug of hot coffee, most of the junior officers were directed to some lorries. With great joy and just in the nick of time I spotted a colleague of mine from the cadet days. He was getting ready to set off in his own Citroen. I yelled: " Richard! Wait a minute!". Grabbing my little case and the attaché case I dashed across to him to find out whether there would be room for me. He was pleased to see me and even more pleased to offer me a seat in his sports coupe. He admitted later that his generosity was partly based on ulterior motives. More than once his little car had been under threat of being commandeered by some senior officer for "official use". Now, with two of us in it there would be no room for "official" passengers. We joined the general stream of traffic. We did not get very far however - there was a loud bang...we had a puncture! There was no such luxury as spare tyres! As if that was not enough, when jacking the car up, Richard noticed that another tyre was almost flat! I must admit that when I first saw his car I thought it had rather a tired look about it. On the other hand, that might have protected him from being commandeered with a stronger effect than his prowess in evasion.

Two tyres were too much to cope with at this time of night - it was past midnight. Richard would not leave his car so he stretched himself as well as he could across the seats and I had to bang on the door of a nearby house. I was admitted by an ancient Jewess who became quite hospitable after some explanations on my part. She offered me a cup of hot milk and very decent accommodation. I still do not know her name but I'll call her Rachel since that was not the only night I had to spend there.

In the morning we were finishing the repair job when a kind of Jeep pulled up near to us and who should be driving it? Zygmunt! - another friend from the same year of my Cadet intake. Our reunion had to be brief as Zyg was in a hurry to keep up with his unit. The strange thing was that he was also heading in the opposite direction to us! When we remarked on this he simply shrugged his shoulders saying:

"I've got to go with my squadron wherever the Leader decides".

We had noticed that there have been two streams of traffic resolutely going in opposite directions for a while. This created a picture in my mind of mice trapped against a wall and running along the skirting board hither and thither trying to find a way out of the trap. The repairs completed we had some refreshments. Whilst munching some bread and sipping milk we discussed our situation and what was more important - our future. Zygmunt's remarks and our own observations had caused some doubt in our minds about the wisdom of our direction of travel. So taking the path of "least resistance" our unanimous decision was to stay put for at least a day and "see". If nothing else transpired at least we would have had a rest. We lazed about all day.

In the evening the whole area for miles around was covered

with men in uniforms looking for a peaceful corner. Anywhere... like pubs, cafés, restaurants, schools and even churches. I was already assessing some barns and even trees for possible shelter when I decided to try old Rachel again - bless her heart. After Richard managed to hide his car behind a shed she gave us a decent meal before settling us down for the night in two very comfortable beds.

We still could not see our way clear by the next day but in the afternoon our "wanderlust" returned and we moved on towards Zaleszczyki, which we found just as thoroughly swamped with blue uniforms. Eventually we managed to obtain a corner in a farmer's barn for the night. One of the first men I saw as we emerged from the barn was Colonel Haberek. I knew him as a helpful senior officer so I made a beeline for him and without much ado stated my desire to locate and rejoin my small band of men as they must have been somewhere in this overcrowded corner of Poland.

"Maybe they are near Sniatyn?" I suggested.

As it happened he was planning to go in that direction so he offered me a lift. I dashed back to Richard, explained my plan and, grabbing my belongings, wished him safe and successful travel. Before nightfall I was back in the village where I was welcomed once again by the kind Rachel. To my delight the colonel was still prepared to carry me towards Sniatyn the next morning. It was September 17th. We reached our target about noon and started looking for the railway station. As we were crossing a high bridge over a river I spotted two N.C.O.s in Air-Force uniforms walking in the opposite direction and I recognised Sgt Galuszek. To my joy he told me that most of the P.R.2 men were in this village. The colonel smiled with satisfaction as he handed me my luggage. We shook hands, which was remarkable considering the difference of ranks, and he drove off whilst Sgt Galuszek led me to a field just outside the village. We were greeted by shouts: "Our Lieutenant is here!" and in no time I was surrounded by a crowd of men trying to tell me all at once what had happened to them since we had parted and at the same time asking me about my experiences. I was glad and proud to find them all in good spirits and really pleased with their quite obvious joy at our reunion.

The P.R.2 was rather depleted in numbers of men and transport but thanks to perspicacity of the N.C.O.s enough lorries had been recovered including the one with our private luggage...including my larger case containing the rest of my worldly possessions! In the meantime our infallible cook produced lunch on his mobile field kitchen and immediately after we witnessed another air raid. They were bombing the railway station. Wagons were thrown about like match boxes and set on fire but the sight of this destruction and the blast of the bombs did not make much impression on us any more. It was becoming a way of life, just like the constant travelling; not knowing where one was going to spend the next night.

There were some rumours that English planes had been delivered to Romania for our Air Force and all we had to do was get there and collect them. It sounded very simple. Too simple! Leaving out all the practical difficulties of the conversion of pilots, retraining of maintenance crews, of supplies bombs and ammunition there was an obvious political snag. Romania was bound by an alliance with Poland but at the same time she was in deadly danger from the Germans glowering menacingly from across the Czechoslovakian border. Accepting military equipment for Poland would most certainly have precipitated a hostile reaction from the Nazis.

My deliberations of this problem were suddenly blasted aside by one of the corporals running from the village shouting:

"The Russians are coming with their tanks!"

Apparently the Soviet troops had crossed our eastern borders and their tanks were moving in our direction. It was amazing how, to a man, everybody took this as a hostile gesture and not as neighbours coming to help. Within minutes our convoy was ready to move once again and the leading lorry nearly collided with a motorcyclist who came with orders for immediate evacuation towards the Romanian border. We joined a massive stream of motorised vehicles, horse-drawn carts and pedestrians - all desperately trying to get out of the trap that was fast closing in on us. We picked up a few civilians and, by an amazing coincidence, one of them was my Professor of Mathematics and another, a young Polish count, whom I had previously met in the college where he did his short training as a reservist.

Present day Eastern Europe with places referred to in the text

Leaving our Homeland Behind

We would not be allowed to enter neutral Romania bearing arms. Heart-breaking moments and scenes followed - we were leaving our Fatherland for Heaven only knows how long and, to turn the knife in the wound, we were ordered to dump our arms in a heap. With tears in my eyes I had to pull my pistol out of its holster and throw it on to the tangled mass of rifles, pistols, bayonets and even light machine guns. Men shuffled sadly, holding their heads down dejectedly as if trying to avoid being seen committing such a dishonourable deed as throwing their arms on the ground. Our rifles - which were "more important to us and better looked after than our sweethearts" according to the sergeants who trained us - were now just a heap of scrap metal! Our miserable thoughts were interrupted by a sudden order to cross the border and follow a Romanian officer's vehicle who would lead us to our internment camp. Where and how far - we had no idea.

A couple of hours later we reached Czerniowce where we were to spend the night. Next morning we received our pay with war allowances, etc - all in Polish Zloty! In consequence, there was a tremendous rush to the banks with everybody trying to exchange them for Romanian ley. Those who managed to get into the banks found that the exchange rate was falling even whilst they were queuing and only a very limited amount was accepted for exchange! I do not know what agreement has been made between the Romanian and the Polish governments but this was a complete shambles. We knew that gold reserves had left the country together with the government but we were seeing very little benefit of that gold.

Having had one of those nights on a mattress of a single straw thickness I felt more drowsy than usual and must have fallen asleep. The noise of the lorry's engine and the constant wobbling of my body made me feel that I was travelling not in a lorry but on a train for some strange reason. What really gave me a shock was that I could suddenly see my mother and father, my brother and my sister, just a little baby in the arms of our maid. We were all trying to sleep but only the baby and my two-year old brother, Genio, were succeeding. I was trying to understand where we were going and why my whole family were with me.

My mind was struggling to unravel the puzzle: "Why do I see this kind of picture? I know that I am travelling in a lorry and not in a train."

My mind had thrown me almost 20 years back to when I was about four and a half years of age, to an almost identical situation when we were trying to escape being captured by the advancing Bolshevik army.

"Who is chasing us?" I growled, half asleep. The thought that we are being followed by the enemy made me open my eyes. We were in the same position as before, behind the Romanian officer. Nothing had changed.

"I've only just wakened up. Is everything all right?" I asked my driver.

"Yes Sir, but you tried to shout something I could not understand" he answered looking rather puzzled.

"Oh, I dreamed that I was on a train with my family. When I was only about four years old we had to escape from the Bolsheviks. Just like today."

He was quite obviously interested to hear more but I reduced the story to just a couple of sentences as I felt that it was more important to keep our minds on the task in hand.

"I'll tell you more - if you are still interested - when we settle down in the camp. I have a feeling that we are going to stay there for a while."

The progress of our convoy was very slow and some days we did not move at all. We had no idea what our destination was to be. My mind was gradually relaxing, having been relieved of the duties and responsibilities of a young officer in charge of the P.R.2 unit with all the lorries, machines and materials for aircraft repair and, most importantly, the men. The torturing worries of those 17 days and nights in Poland were fading away. All I had to do now was to make sure that we followed the Romanian officer.

Fortunately our "host", the Romanian Government, was obliged to keep us alive ie: to supply some food and to provide some kind of accommodation. This was often in sheds, barns or even in schools, with a layer of straw as a mattress. Our own Government, on the other hand, was allowed to pay us part of our wages. Unfortunately, this was in Polish currency, which we then had to try to change into Romanian ley and to be able to do this we had to stop in a town with a bank in it, not an easy task, given our route. Now, try to imagine 30 or more men rushing into the bank to obtain at least the minimum ration in ley before the bank declares that it cannot exchange any more. To make it even more frustrating we never got the official rate of exchange. With this money we could buy some fruit, or just improve our rations and those who so badly needed cigarettes got them.

In these conditions morale and discipline would collapse in a couple of days. It was important to preserve some semblance of a fighting force and so morning parades were ordered and according to our custom we sang the morning hymn "When the dawn is rising". On the first day, immediately after the morning hymn, someone with a powerful voice intoned a hymn that could be considered to be our second national anthem. It was taken up by us all, with a heart-rending cry: "A free Fatherland please return to us, O Lord."

This was not singing. It was a sobbing, groaning noise; a frightful sound made by hundreds of constricted throats mourning their dead, their enslaved and their raped country. We felt less and less like soldiers and more like refugees; pushed ahead, stopped, herded into some buildings and told to make ourselves "at home". I was much more at home under a tree in the Polish Woods. We were kept alive on handouts of foul soup and bread. By now the exchange facilities had completely broken down - the banks no longer wanted to see us.

Two days later we moved on towards Bucuresti (Bucharest), the capital, which looked more promising. To our dismay our stop there lasted only as long as it takes to put a few hundred men on a train. Then off again on a longish journey until we reached a camp near a town called Campulung. The surrounding scenery was very pretty with the Transylvanian Alps looking down on our camp. This was to be our home for the foreseeable future. Thus, on September 23rd we became internees.

The camp facilities were dismal. When all those allocated to that camp arrived there must have been over 800 of us crowded in one long two-storey block of old fashioned barracks with the command offices in a low building on the other side of the parade ground. A fence topped with barbed wire surrounded the whole camp and armed guards were stationed at the gates and other strategic points. We felt like prisoners! Our own Commanding Officer had the most difficult task of trying to retain some semblance of discipline and still pay lip service to the usual rules of internment whilst we, the "inmates", were far from being reconciled to our fate. All sorts of plots and ideas started germinating almost on the first day - more about that later!

Within days it was obvious that hygiene would be our major problem. Washing facilities were very primitive and the lavatories stopped functioning one by one. Our complaints to the Romanian Commandant through our Commanding Officer had no effect. The result of "no action" was that the small woods within the camp perimeter rapidly became a stinking mess. The efforts to build field lavatories were thwarted by the reluctance to supply spades or any disinfectant or even lime.

About a week later something strange happened. After the morning parade we were told to collect our towels and assemble in groups of forty on the parade ground. From there we were marched, under guard of course, to the railway station. We could not see the connection between our towels and the railway station until we found ourselves in front of a short train consisting of wagons converted into showers. We had to leave our clothes outside and then scramble into the steaming wagons. Oh joy! Hot water streaming from a dozen jets! There was a lot of scrubbing and singing. Most of us were quite content to wash our hair and bodies but some had the excellent idea of jumping out for their underwear, putting it on and giving it a wash in that novel way. I get hot and bothered at the mere thought of it now, knowing as I do of similar showers used by the Nazis in some concentration camps.

Our return to barracks was accompanied by song and cheer. This changed to jubilation when two announcements were made: one, the shower train would come once a week and two, Officers and N.C.O.s would be allowed to march to the nearby town for their main meals - at their own expense and under guard, of course. It was surprising how many managed to obtain those unobtainable ley.

After three or four visits to town we could see the possibilities that were open to us by such relaxation in our camp restrictions. On one of these excursions Peter and I decided to take a look at the countryside towards Yugoslavia. We climbed a small hill from which we had beautiful views in three directions but towards the west and Yugoslavia there was a forbidding-looking range of mountains. Returning to our camp much later than the main party we decided to test the guards and to march boldly through the gates as if it was the normal routine. Nobody stopped us and no questions were asked.

Later we heard that others, especially the men who were not included in the "privileged diners" group, made similar tests resorting to simple bribery, which proved to be the most infallible method. Another way was to test the guards' ignorance of their own weapons. The trick was to approach the guard with smiles offering a cigarette or chocolate and then to admire his rifle so obviously that the proud guard would let one handle it! Imagine parting with one's rifle! For that, during my training days, one would most certainly collect a week's C.B. (confined to barracks) or even imprisonment. Anyway, with sounds of amazement and excitement one would turn the rifle this way and that, whilst at the same time releasing the catch holding the breach-block in position. After that one would pig-headedly pull the breach-block right back, which to the guard's complete surprise would come right out of the rifle. With convincing display of embarrassment one would then hand the rifle back to the nonplussed guard who had no idea how to reassemble the pieces. He was now unable to challenge the trickster and his friends who were now marching out or raise the alarm by firing a shot. There was an element of risk involved because one never knew when a better-trained chap would be on guard duties. Also one could count on this trick not being reported for another reason...the punishment.

After only a week a few "inmates" disappeared. This was not a matter for discussion, so we only wished them well and secretly started working out our own schemes of escape. Somehow our Senior Officer got to know about this line in private enterprise and he immediately let it be known that nothing must be undertaken without his blessing.

Getting out of the camp was comparatively easy, as illustrated above. However, quite apart from the language difficulties, outside the camp there was nothing and nobody who would support a fugitive unless he had an inexhaustible supply of ley (cash). In such a position, he would have an excellent chance of being robbed. First the fugitive would have to get to Bucharest, the capital, about 100 miles away. There he would then have to find the Polish Embassy which was still functioning in order to obtain a passport of some sort and instructions for the next step. Meanwhile our orders were: "Be patient and wait your turn."

One day the Romanian camp Commandant failed to appear for the morning parade. This in itself did not mean anything special to us but when the next morning a much less pleasant face accepted the adjutant's daily report we were curious to find out more about him. What we discovered was not to our liking! The previous Commandant with a truly Romanian name like Badulescu, was replaced by a Major Zank [pronounced Tzank] - a very Germanic-sounding name. We braced ourselves for a much more rigorous regime but to our surprise only the morning count became more meticulous: the dining-out was allowed to continue. Now we had to be much more careful about the "top up the numbers" game. The parade took place in front of our block of barracks and the line of men stretched from one end of the building to the other. When the Romanian officer was counting heads somewhere near the middle the required number of chaps from the top of the line had to run back behind the barracks and unobtrusively join the far end thus presenting the correct total. Our worry was that one day there would be two or three too many!

Very soon after the change of Commandants a group of about 30 of the internees quite brazenly declared themselves to be of German origin and demanded either immediate repatriation or preferential treatment at the very least. Unfortunately for them our own men were the first to know about their aspirations. We, at the officers' end of the building, only heard some subdued commotion and a lot of toing and froing between the main block and a hut behind it. Apparently an immediate isolation of the "Germans" had been carried out and a virtual imprisonment made within the camp. Their hut was amply big enough but the hygiene facilities were even worse than ours. Our own facilities by then were quite primitive and we had to trek past this hut into the much "over-fertilised" woods for our natural needs.

At least twice a week a liaison officer from the Polish Embassy or Air-Force H.Q. would visit our camp to consult with our Senior Officer and at the same time to visit the camp Commandant, usually with the idea of obtaining some improvement in food, hygiene etc. A much more important part of his mission was to collect the photographs of the next group approved for escape. We had professional photographers amongst us who never parted with their equipment so there was no problem with a passport size photo except that it had to be of a civilian - one jacket and tie served hundreds of men admirably. I soon armed myself with a set of photos and eagerly awaited a nod or a wink from the Senior Officer or his adjutant. In the meantime I had to obtain a civvy outfit. This could be achieved by selling anything of value whilst on one of the lunchtime outings and buying all sorts of clothing rubbish as long as it was civilian. So my beautiful leather coat, my lifesaver on so many cold nights, had to go in exchange for civvy trousers and jacket and a wide-brimmed hat. This left me with a few hundred ley for the journey itself.

The day came when two other officers and I were informed that our photographs and full details were required before the next visit of the liaison officer. We had to think of some suitable non-military occupation for that purpose. I decided to be a student. We knew that within a few days of the liaison officer's departure, our passports would be ready and waiting for us in Bucharest. It was up to us to get there, collect documents and instructions and set off on the next stage of our escape. The three of us decided to stick together and agreed on the day and mode of transport. Wladek, who maintained that he had picked up enough Romanian to bargain with a taxi driver, was given a sum of ley and the commission to get the taxi for 19:30hrs next evening.

I wore my civvies under my uniform when going out for lunch that day. I smuggled the rest of my essential possessions in a small attaché case and a colleague obligingly carried another small case. The guards did not take much notice of our luggage since we had been in and out many times before with cases carrying fruit, food and all sorts of purchases. In the restaurant near the food counter I saw Wladek. He gave me a broad wink to indicate that everything was in order. Our third man, Bronek, was in another corner with a bulging case under his chair. Bronek and I pre-arranged to meet after dark in a quiet part of the town and Wladek would come in the taxi at the agreed hour to pick us up. In the meantime we had to get enough food inside us to last us until the next day.

When my tummy, filled with excitement rather than food, said "enough" I disappeared into the outside toilet block. There I discarded my uniform knowing that it would be immediately picked up and returned to camp where it would be altered and adapted for sale to raise cash for someone else. I made my way from there towards a park where I spent what seemed like endless hours walking, sitting on benches and trying to look like a young Romanian enjoying a sunny afternoon. Watching the sun setting behind the mountains, I chewed an apple and a piece of bread and started looking round for any shady character who might be Bronek in disguise. At last it was time to proceed to the appointed corner. I arrived with about three minutes to spare. No sign of Bronek! Ten minutes later a taxi arrived and pulled up nearby. I was delighted to see Wladek jump out but at the same time I was worried that Bronek was nowhere to be seen and we had agreed that only fifteen minutes would be allowed for latecomers. At 19:40 we had the last look round – still no sign of Bronek. Obviously he could not make it for some reason. We hopped into the car and moved off.

A few miles outside the town, to our surprise, the driver stopped and asked for 100 ley in advance. This made us rather suspicious but by using a few words of German and a lot of sign language he made it clear to us that there were two roadblocks ahead of us. One only a few minutes further on and the other just before Bucharest. The money was needed to get us through the "Soldatul" controls so we had no choice but to give him the money. When he stopped again only a few minutes later, we anxiously peered into the darkness. There was nothing to be seen. The driver got out and signalled that we should come out as well. He pointed along the road and said: "Soldatul", which in most languages has the same meaning. At the same time he opened the boot of the taxi and indicated that he expected us to get in and stay there until we had passed through the control point

Fortunately this was a roomy Chevrolet so I did not find it unbearable but Wladek who was 6ft 6ins and of big frame, had to be pushed down with the lid of the boot. The taxi moved off again and after a few minutes it slowed down to a stop. We heard a challenge: "Apreste! [stop]", followed by a noisy exchange between our driver and somebody who did not sound convinced by the replies. Next we heard the passenger door open, some mumbling and the door shut again. Any second now the boot would be opened…nothing happened except for some more shouting and then the taxi started to move. We hardly dared to breathe or move. Our joints were getting stiffer by the minute. At last we stopped and the lid flew open and we could clamber out. It took us a few minutes to straighten out and sort out the creases in our knees and necks.

After about an hour's travelling we stopped again expecting to repeat the performance of folding our bodies into a small compartment. Instead, the driver indicated that this was as far as he was prepared to take us and put his hand out for the rest of the fare. We could see the glow of the city reflected in the high cloud and some scattered lights below so we knew it was not too far to walk. But what about the second roadblock, the "Soldatul" and the bribe he had collected in advance? We gave him the fare, minus 50 ley and we left him standing and swearing; at least, that is what it sounded like to us. We had a mile or two in front of us and midnight was fast approaching, so we set off at a brisk pace, keeping a sharp look out for the control point. Either we were in luck or there was no control on this road and after at least an hour the sleepy suburbs changed to more business-like parts of the city and soon we saw a hotel. Even though it was very late the hotel was still open and we had no difficulty in getting a room. So the first part of our escape was successfully concluded but locating the Polish Embassy gave us some anxious thoughts to go to bed with. Our tired bodies demanded sleep and that was what they got regardless of the uncertainty of the next day.

We knew the name of the street that the Embassy was on but had no idea how to find it. Eating our breakfast rolls and drinking coffee, we decided to risk it and to write the address on a piece of paper and approach the receptionist. It was so obvious we were not the first to point to a street name on a piece of paper that we could have laughed. The street map was in front of us in a flash and the kind receptionist gave us very clear directions. There were many people on the streets by now, so we did not feel too vulnerable. Our breakfast was too sketchy for our needs and every time we passed a cafe or a restaurant we felt an irresistible pull. As we were about to pass the third cafe we performed a smart left turn, marched in and ordered bread, sausages and coffee. It was good and, as it turned out, a very wise move.

By mid-morning we had found the "street" and the first thing that struck us was the number of silent figures, wearing hats pulled well down over their faces, all proceeding towards the same building. At the door we were quite cheerfully greeted in Polish and told to take our places in the queue. The queue started almost at the front door and disappeared up a staircase on which sat at least two dozen men, either half-asleep or deep in conversation. They were probably describing their "most daring escape" of the century to each other.

It was about 3.00pm when we got to within sight of the all-important door. An hour later I was facing a weary official sitting behind a heap of files and a box-full of folded documents. When I gave him my name he consulted a long list and then pulled out one of the documents. For the purpose of the travel document I had given my mother's family name (which, by the way, did not change my initials) and felt a little disappointed when he addressed me by my true name. So much for conspiracy! Next, he read out my occupation: "Farmer". I tried to stop him and to explain that I did not know the first thing about gardening let alone farming but he took no notice, just waved his arm and quoted the rest of the details on it as if to satisfy himself of what a good job he had done. Before I could open my mouth he blurted out:

"You have a passport so consider yourself lucky. Here it is and in that envelope there is money and further instructions. Please let the next one in."

I pocketed the papers and went out leaving the door open for Wladek and sat down to wait for him. Just to make sure that I had heard the clerk right I started reading his description of myself. My name was the one I had chosen as my "nome de guerre". That was the only thing to agree with the details I had given on the form in the camp. Pretending to be a farmer would be a simple thing when compared with the rest of the details - "blue eyes" and "blonde hair" whereas I had brown eyes and almost black hair! To make matters worse I had to stretch myself by at least 10 centimetres to fit my stated dimensions. I did not know whether to swear or to laugh.

When Wladek came out we found that our instructions were identical: "Catch the morning train, 8:45 to Constanta, change at Medgidia for Bazardzik thence by bus to Balchic". The fact that we did not need to separate cheered me up. We marched out looking for a not-too-posh restaurant - it was well past 5:00pm and we were starving. After a decent meal we decided to locate the railway station and then a cheap hotel not too far away. It was '"early to bed boys" that night: partly to make up for the previous night and partly because we did not much like the idea of being seen.

The morning found us refreshed and in good spirits. We returned to the same cafe for a substantial breakfast - the lesson of the previous day was firmly implanted in our memories. Next - shopping for food for the journey and by then it was time to direct our steps to the station. Although it was barely 8.15 the train was already in so we started looking for an empty compartment. There were no coaches with compartments, just a string of "open plan" coaches with wooden benches and all of these were half full already. We sat down by a door and pretended to be too tired to keep our eyes open and I kept a watch on our co-passengers and the newcomers from under my eyelashes. They all seemed very tired and uncommunicative – just as if a nightshift of workers was leaving the town. Here and there somebody whispered or mumbled something to his neighbour but otherwise they gave the impression of a most unsociable crowd.

At last the doors were slammed shut, whistles shrilled, the locomotive hooted and we were off. Many of the sleepy faces came briefly to life with their eyes darting left and right as if to make sure that we were moving in the right direction. Then, as the rattle of the wheels increased the whispers and mumbles changed to quite loud talk. To my surprise these roughly clad peasants who looked very Romanian were speaking Polish! I kicked Wladek's foot and winked at him inviting him to listen.

"Looks as if the whole train was specially laid on for us" he said.

"There is more safety in numbers" I agreed, "But it would be quite unbelievable if the railway police did not know what was going on."

Soon the Polish language was heard quite openly from all parts of the coach. So, joking and comparing notes we reached Medgidia station where we were to change trains. As we slowed down everybody was busy getting down their bundles and cases and those nearer to doors started operating the door handles, but as they looked out they saw the platform lined with troops armed with rifles and with bayonets fixed. As I had feared, this mass exodus of quaintly clad people, all behaving suspiciously, could not possibly go unnoticed.

Then a most amazing mass thought communication took place. To a man we turned about and used the opposite doors to scramble into a train standing very conveniently on the next platform. There must have been a couple of hundred of us but the manoeuvre was executed very quickly and efficiently. A few people were already in the second train but they did not show the least interest in us or in our method of entry. We had no idea where this train was going or when it was due to leave. It might even take us back to Bucharest!...but anything was better than being marched under guard to some barracks or prison and then transported back to Campulung.

As we again tried to become as unnoticeable as possible the train started moving without the usual banging doors and whistling. At least the decision "to stay or get out" was taken out of our hands and we were pleased to notice that we continued to travel east, ie: towards the Black Sea. Soon we should reach the point where the train would have to turn either south or north. North would spell disaster...that way lay Poland, now occupied by Russia. South would suit us because that way was our destination - the little town of Balchic. Our worries were needless as we soon discovered from the other passengers on the train. They were all like us – Polish airmen in disguise on their way to Balchic.

I could not believe that all this was due to sheer luck. On reflection, I could not remember seeing any genuine Romanians on the first train and for the second train to stand so conveniently and move off so promptly could have only been due to good organisation and lots and lots of the omnipotent bribes. At this rate we should be on our way to the Middle East or Egypt or France in a few days. Who knows where? As long as it was out of the grasp of the Germans or Russians and towards another chance to fight!

Later in the afternoon the sea appeared on our left and half an hour later the train stopped. All the doors were opened with a command in Polish:

"Wysiadac!" ("All change!").

The whole station had been taken over by the Polish Authorities and they even had a convoy of buses lined up for us. An hour later we were in the square of the town of Balchic. We were ordered to surrender our passports and in exchange were given slips of paper with addresses in the village. These addresses were to be our quarters.

The little town was quite attractive, stretching along a large bay on the Black Sea, with fine houses, hotels and even mansions overlooking the beaches. Within a couple of hours we had had a good meal, and had settled down in our allocated billets where, to my delight, I found a group of colleagues from the same intake from the Air Force Commissioning School. Naturally, there was no inclination to sleep until well after midnight.

There was not much to the next day after exploring the immediate vicinity, except to wait for the parade in the afternoon when we expected to hear some news about our next move. However, there was no news of any move for the next few days and we were told that patience was the order of the day.

"Recuperate, rest and stand by for action at very short notice!".

Those orders were given in a market square dominated by a mosque with an imposing minaret.

A shortage of reading matter resulted in card schools springing up everywhere. I had a good refresher course in bridge with such experts as Adam, Zygmunt, Rys and others. This "holiday" lasted eight whole days when at last the peace was rudely shattered by a call to an immediate parade and the news that a ship was coming to take us to another theatre of war. Could it be France, Egypt or Syria...who knows where?

Our passports were returned to us and so we thought it was only a question of packing and lining up for embarkation...that would be too simple for the local Romanian Customs Officers. They could not let such a "golden" opportunity, in the full meaning of the word "gold", slip by. We were expected to obtain their "Viasul Placari" (at least, that is what it sounded like) which was something equivalent to an Exit Visa. This could be given only to those who could prove a non-military past. How does one convince them that whatever occupation was stated on the passport was the job one has been doing for the last few or many years, depending on one's age? Those who were not sure held back and let the older or obviously unfit men go first. Physical disability would be the most convincing proof. Suddenly there were scores of young men limping around, or gazing into space with a vacant look as if their sight had failed, or asking people to repeat louder whatever was said to them. One fellow decided that his mental faculties were far below the minimum military standard and laid on a performance so convincing that we earnestly began to fear for the state of his mind. It took him many days to persuade his friends that it was only an act. Unfortunately, these ploys only worked in a few cases. Many came back from the interview very cross because of the red stamp in the right hand corner of the passport which meant: no Exit Visa!

An industry of erasing such stamps developed within minutes when someone with skill and experience in getting round bureaucracy suggested rubbing that particular corner with soap before going for the interview. This worked beautifully. All one had to do was to scrape off the thin layer of soap together with the obnoxious stamp and try again. This put heart into the less courageous souls and I went along with them only to get the red stamp treatment myself.

There was one foolproof method available to some of us ie: those who were in possession of funds. Fold a high denomination banknote into the passport and "Hey Presto!" Without any questions and often without even looking up from the space between his knees and the table the official would slap on the Exit Visa stamp.

After a week of leisurely holiday with bridge and poker going in many corners we changed from a classless society to two classes; the "haves" and the "have-nots", meaning: those "who have or not have" the visas. My lessons in bridge had been rather costly so I had to face the customs officials again and again.

I was near despair seeing more and more men going on board... many of them my bridge instructors. This went on until the morning parade on November 5th when the ship was moved away from the quay and anchored a few hundred metres away. Our passports were collected again and we were assured that soon there would be another transport. We were not quite satisfied with these promises but on the other hand even our inexperienced eyes in maritime matters could see that the ship with the name "Patris" was not really big enough to provide the usual accommodation for those lucky ones already on board. But every one of us had a similar thought in mind: "Surely there would be room for just one more, even if I had to stand all the way!" With these thoughts in mind, we were sent to lunch.

Sometime in the afternoon a special parade was called. Our chief announced that a passport draw would take place and the first twenty lucky ones would have their passports returned and be allowed to get on board on the strict condition that the customs men did not see or hear anything. It was a plot between our "management" and the ship's captain. No doubt this cost the "management" a few thousand ley. To my utter disbelief my name came up together with many of my fellow engineers. This kind of luck had a dubious appearance about it - after I had a good look at the jubilant faces stepping out to collect the document - but who would want to question it?

A few years later, when I was older, better informed and had time to think about it, this daring plan appeared very wise. Our high ranking officers must have already looked a few years ahead to the day of victory and to the urgent needs of our country. Reconstruction would have a high priority and a number of educated, professional people would be "worth their weight in gold!"

What they could not foresee was that the last ally to join us in the struggle would be very useful but at the same time very greedy and would thwart all such hopes. Our Leaders' proposals, taken to the final negotiations by Mr Churchill, would be rejected by the other two negotiators - one of them (Stalin) ruthlessly selfish and the other (Roosevelt) in a bad state of health.

Our group met for a short consultation and we quickly agreed a plan that would require a largish boat and the co-operation of one of the local fishermen. The suggestion of swimming over to the ship was never taken seriously and the idea of stealing a boat was shot down since it would antagonise the locals and would make things difficult for our comrades forced to remain here for a little longer. Each of us had to contribute a certain amount of money, which was pooled and given to two elected men. They sounded more confident in German and had a few words of Romanian so they were elected as our negotiators and sent to the far end of the village where we had noticed some fishing activities. About an hour later the emissaries returned with smiling faces and a bargain. A boat would come to the far side of the quay at 23.00 hrs, that side of the quay being out of sight from the customs hut. We should get there without attracting anybody's attention and then do as we were told. Our negotiators had to give the fisherman a quarter of the agreed sum in advance, the rest would be payable when the last man got on board the ship.

Well before the appointed time one could observe shadowy figures slipping out of their billets and sneaking away in the poorly lit streets - all in the same direction. All of us were gathered by half past ten, crouching in almost complete darkness under the pier and clutching our luggage. All ears were straining to hear the first sounds of a boat. The water was very calm with not even small wavelets to produce a faint sound of a splash now and then. The minutes dragged by painfully and the tension was rising with furtive whispers and the shuffling of feet. Suddenly someone with sharper hearing than most whispered: "Shush...Listen!" Then we could hear the muffled rumble of oars in the rowlocks and the gentle, rhythmical splash of water. Another minute and the keel of a boat crunched into the gravel. We were told to take off our shoes and be prepared to wade in up to our knees before boarding. First our negotiators went aboard - their reward being almost dry feet but for that they had to stow away our belongings passed on to them. Next they had to go astern to relieve the bow to make it easier for the rest of us to push the boat out a little. Carefully keeping it afloat we boarded one by one. Our bare feet did not make any noise, which would have echoed far and wide in the stillness of the night. The last one in got more than his knees wet but the boat stayed afloat and we were ready to go.

As soon as we rounded the head of the pier a string of lights became visible in the distance indicating the position of the "Patris", which in English is "Fatherland". Was it "the Fate" playing cruel jokes with us or was she already hinting that this was our first step towards our Fatherland? One of the ferrymen indicated that we should make ourselves as invisible as possible by sitting on the wet bottom of the boat because of the searchlight that fortunately never stabbed the perfect darkness around us. It must have been about midnight when we reached the ship and we had to proceed to the side invisible from the land. There we found a landing platform with a seaman waiting for us. He made the boat fast and helped us to get out and then we formed a human 'chain' up to the deck passing up our luggage first. Our negotiators, after paying off the ferrymen, were the last to get up on deck and were greeted by grateful handshakes and shoulder slaps.

The next thing was to find somewhere to rest our tired bodies and this proved rather difficult. The ship had cabins and there were berths for about 350 passengers but there were over 1500 of us! Our group scattered all over the ship looking for likely corners and I was lucky to find one of my bridge partners who took me to his four-berth cabin. There were already five occupants, with one of them on the floor that was barely wide enough for two bodies, so I had little room to stretch and possibly to sleep. What if one of higher-up passengers should decide to jump onto the floor during the night? Still, beggars cannot be choosers and I was grateful to be accepted into the already overcrowded cabin. Whilst we were settling down there was a lot of chain clanging, the engines went into full power and we were off!

I soon went to sleep and did not wake up until broad daylight. Most of my companions were already out so I jumped up to look out of the porthole and could clearly see a coastline. We were rather close to it and I excitedly concluded that we were going into the straits of the Bosphorus. Big and small boats were everywhere and houses clearly visible on the Turkish coast. This was too interesting to be viewed from a porthole so I made for the deck. As soon as I opened the door I was met by a heavy cloud of stale air - in our cabin we at least had a porthole, which would be kept open unless the sea became too rough but the poor fellows sleeping in the passageways had none. Nor chance to admire the view or to let some fresh air in. There were still quite a few bodies on the floor which made my progress difficult but fortunately the sea was calm. The fresh air on top was delicious and the views on both sides highly fascinating.

When we entered the Sea of Marmara the pretty coastline, together with its scenery, receded and it was time to look for breakfast. To our disgust this was not included in our passage, which meant that we had to pay for every morsel of bread and every cup of coffee. After scratching about for the last ley for the ferrymen I did not have enough for one proper breakfast. My good friend Zyg (a very good bridge player!) came to my rescue but how was I going to manage during the rest of the voyage? I need not have worried for as soon as we got through the Dardanelles, the sea decided to show us its nastier face. It started blowing and throwing the small ship about. It was not a liner and was obviously overloaded with human cargo at the top and not enough freight lower down to steady it a little. By evening I had had enough of beautiful scenery - all I wanted was to lie down and try to control my first horrible experience of seasickness. Most of my pals felt likewise so there was no more grumbling about having to pay for every scrap of food. All we wanted now was less swaying and rolling. We again attempted to leave the porthole open. After about half an hour of chatting we settled down.

I was roused from my sleep by someone attempting to place his foot rather close to my head. His hand was reaching for the porthole. When I looked at it I thought my eyes were playing tricks. It looked like a very pale grey disc with something like an amazing, shimmering and phosphorescent curtain hanging below it. A curtain of tiny lights cascading to the floor. When I tried to raise myself a little to have a better look I got a shock to feel that my hand was on wet floor. We were rolling so hard that the water was splashing in through the porthole and bringing with it some kind of sea glow-worms. It was fascinating to watch and for a while I just lay admiring the phenomenon. Then my reasoning came to life. Water! In a flash I was getting out of the way of my pal. Fortunately we did not ship too much water or maybe it disappeared through some invisible drain. After an hour or so the air became almost unbreathable with six, mostly sick men in one small cabin.

At last the pale grey disc became light grey and finally dawn began flashing through the glass in rhythm with the ship's rocking. Another hour and my floor mate and I decided that we had had enough so we gathered our toiletries and made for the washroom. The stench in the corridor was appalling and we had to step carefully over the slumbering bodies whilst trying to counteract the violent motion of the ship at the same time. When we reached the toilets we found an indescribable situation in there. The washrooms were not much better - bowls blocked with vomit and water from the taps coming in thin, lazy dribbles. I could not stand this any more so I rushed up the stairs, which to my amazement, were quite clear. They must have proved too uncomfortable for anyone to sleep on. The downwind rail of the deck was thickly populated but I managed to find a slot. I was quite determined that there was no going back to sleeping in the cabin unless the weather calmed down. After a while I felt sufficiently better to leave the sickly company and when I turned round I spotted two of my friends: Wutur (his nickname) and Hrynasz, sitting nearby on a bench in the shelter of the superstructure - both hands firmly gripping the woodwork. They kindly made room for me and we suffered like this for the rest of the day.

By nightfall we all decided that we would not go below, although there was no question of lying down on our bench and very small chance for sleeping. In addition there was the danger of losing one's grip as the inevitable spells of sleepiness overcame us. A length of rope that was hanging above our heads had been irritating us all day by slapping about but now we pulled it down and tied ourselves to the bench. The storm began to get worse. The stars were describing mad semicircles above us and every now and then there was an almighty thump followed by a cascade of spray coming over from the windward side. Above us, on the bridge, we could hear objects rolling about - probably the tins with our rations, which the greedy sailors had kept for themselves.

We must have been semiconscious with sleep when suddenly our bench swung out pivoting on one corner and throwing the other end right against the rail! Hrynasz, who was on my left, took the brunt of the impact but he was a powerful, indestructible fellow. His forearms and shins took the blow. He groaned like a bear and swore like ten troopers. I was in a cold sweat seeing the pale white frothy fingers of the furious sea reaching out for us. What if the rail gave way? We had to push ourselves back to the wall of the superstructure using the rocking motion of the boat to fight gravity. This time we had to use some of the rope to tie the bench itself to the rail which in turn was attached to the superstructure behind us. There was no sleep from now on and our heels were permanently dug in to keep us away from the edge of the deck.

The dawn found us somewhere between Greece and Crete, the fury of the sea abating enough for us to relax and even to leave the bench for a few minutes. We did this one at a time for fear of someone else taking over what we considered our "home". By noon the sun appeared and the deck was quite inviting. Soon we could see sick, pale-looking figures crawling out from the stinking bowels of the ship, stretching their arms and taking deep breaths in the hope of regaining some of their energy from the sun.

Suddenly a commotion ran through us like a wave - a naval vessel was spotted. Friend or foe? She was approaching very fast and soon our "experts" identified her as a British destroyer. Hurrah!! We had some protection at last. A powerful voice projected by the loudhailer said something to the captain of our ship. This brought even the weakest from below the decks so that there was literally standing room only - everybody wanted to see the representative of the mighty Royal Navy. She was a smart, slick ship effortlessly circling round us as if inspecting us from all angles. The loud hailer blasted some very commanding and cross sounding words and then the destroyer streaked off in a westerly direction. At first we had no idea what was said but soon the news filtered down via some linguist. Our excitement exploded as a noisy commentary and speculation - apparently we had been ordered to proceed to Malta. Obviously, when the captain of the destroyer heard [and saw] how many passengers were on board this small ship, he blasted the Greek captain with a few choice words. He promised that the long arm of the Royal Navy would find him on the other side of the world if he chose not to obey the orders immediately. We began to feel like human beings again. Somebody cared about us!

To our astonishment we were told that there would be a meal ready in a couple of hours and we would not have to pay for it! Our

Senior Officer suggested that we should go in groups to eat at half-hourly intervals. Soon afterwards half a dozen surly looking seamen with buckets and brushes appeared from the crew quarters and tried to give the decks a scrub. This proved next to impossible until about a quarter of us got an invitation to go down to queue for the meal. Speculation on what could await us in Malta occupied most of our waking time.

The next day must have been 9th November and the weather was even kinder to us. Many made an attempt at shaving and sprucing themselves up. After some sort of breakfast we settled down to another day of watching the horizon, discussing the possibilities of going to England or of the threat of German U-Boats in the Mediterranean until someone cried out "ZIEMIA!" (Land!). Everybody wanted to see it at the same time and there was a lot of pushing and jostling to find a spot from which one could see the land.

"This must be Malta," shouted out another voice. Malta it was and a couple of hours later our ship was entering the harbour and then gingerly sidled up to a liner tied up at the quay. Our top deck was on the same level as a large door in the side of the liner which opened as soon as we stopped. A kind of a bridge was pushed out of the liner and two men in naval uniforms came over. Two ratings appeared on the bridge barring the entry as if expecting a mad rush across. Actually we did not understand what was going on and so were not in a hurry to go anywhere without some explanation.

Soon enough the word came from our Senior Officer announcing that men belonging to certain units, which he named, were to prepare to change ships. My unit was one of them so I went below deck to collect my gear and then with Hrynasz and most of my cabin mates we just sat on the deck and waited our turn. We finally started moving in a single file to cross the bridge into the liner. There we were met by a sickbay orderly who told us to strip to the waist and move on towards two doctors who gave us a quick inspection with particular attention to the glands under our armpits. Next our names and ranks were noted and we were given a card with the number of the cabin allocated to us. After that we were sent along a labyrinth of corridors to find it.

Hrynasz and I stuck together all the way so when we approached the steward who was allocating the cabins we found we had the same cabin. Not much further along we spotted our number. We opened the door and could not believe our eyes! In front of us was a large, luxuriously finished room with two separate beds and a large window. We dashed in and locked the door, just in case the steward changed his mind. This was luxury!!

A little while later we heard the loudspeakers telling us, in Polish, that showers were now available and that we were expected in the restaurant on deck "B" for the evening meal in one hour. "Wow!". In next to no time we were splashing happily under a stream of warm water. Shaved and brushed we went to look for deck "B" and the restaurant. We were met at the door by a row of smart looking waiters standing to attention to greet a line of scarecrows dressed in a variety of shabby, crumpled and tatty clothes. We felt embarrassed but what could we do? Seated at a long table we were served a first class meal, something we had forgotten existed on this earth. The waiters could not speak Polish and few of us knew any English but we could still feel the warmth and sympathy emanating from these kind men.

The repast over, we went for a stroll to have a look at the other decks and at the island. It was getting too dark so we returned to our cabin only to find the door locked! We could not understand it. We checked the number again and started looking for the steward in charge of our corridor when two Polish officers with a couple of ranks seniority over us, appeared from another cabin. They told us that there had been a mistake and some of the cabins had been re-allocated. We just "happened" to be reallocated to the cabin across the corridor whilst they had the key to our first class cabin. We were told to go in to collect our things and when we did so we found strange cases already installed and our belongings pushed to one side. It took a lot of self control not to say to their faces what we thought of such a sudden "re-allocation" but when we got to our new cabin we let flow a stream of coarse insults towards those who had displaced us. The new room had up-and-down bunks and a space the width of a washbasin, which was opposite the door. Instead of a window we had a jet of air blowing down on us, and it was not fresh air! We settled down for the night amid a lot of grumbling and swearing.

During the next few days we got to know the liner quite well. She was the "Frankonia", a luxury liner, in dock for repairs, which took one whole week. We certainly enjoyed living there, except for the cabin, and enjoyed the Mediterranean autumn but nobody would tell us why we were not allowed to go ashore to see a little of the island. Still - we were much better off than the unfortunate few hundred who had to stay on the "Patris"

At last the repairs were completed and "Frankonia" was made ready to leave Malta. I was convinced that her next port of call would be Liverpool or somewhere in Britain and most of us would have been very pleased to get there. However, decisions made at higher level required us to disembark at Marseilles. Plans were probably already being drawn up to re-enact the historical march of Polish Legions to liberate their Fatherland as we sing about it in our National Anthem, only this time from France and not Italy.

So on a Sunday morning, November 19th 1939, we disembarked at Marseilles and the same day we were on the train for Lyon. The journey was slow and we did not get there until the next morning.

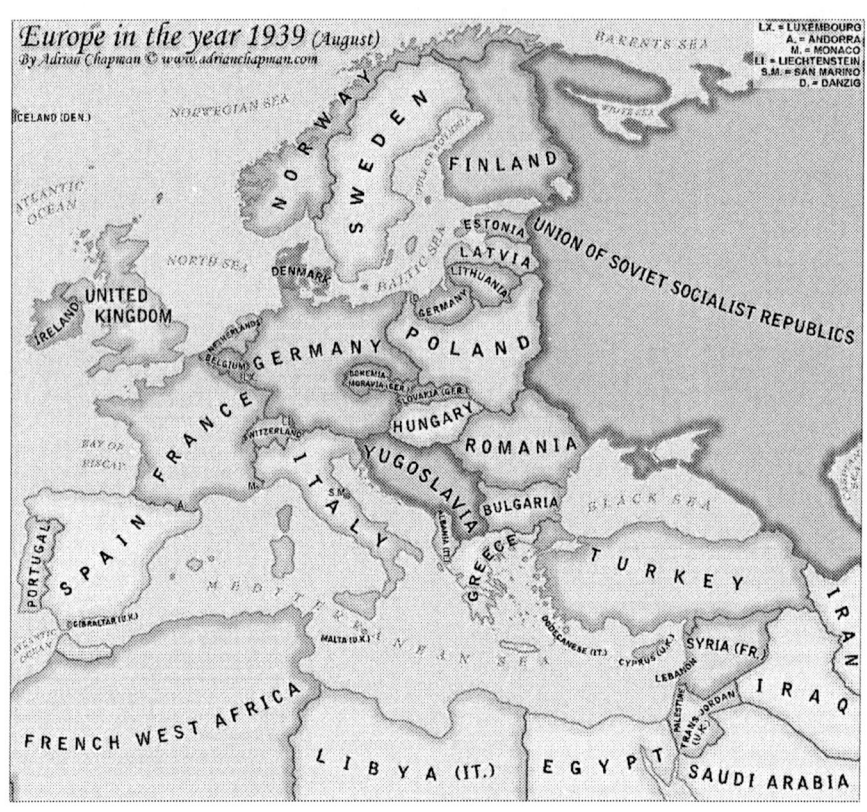

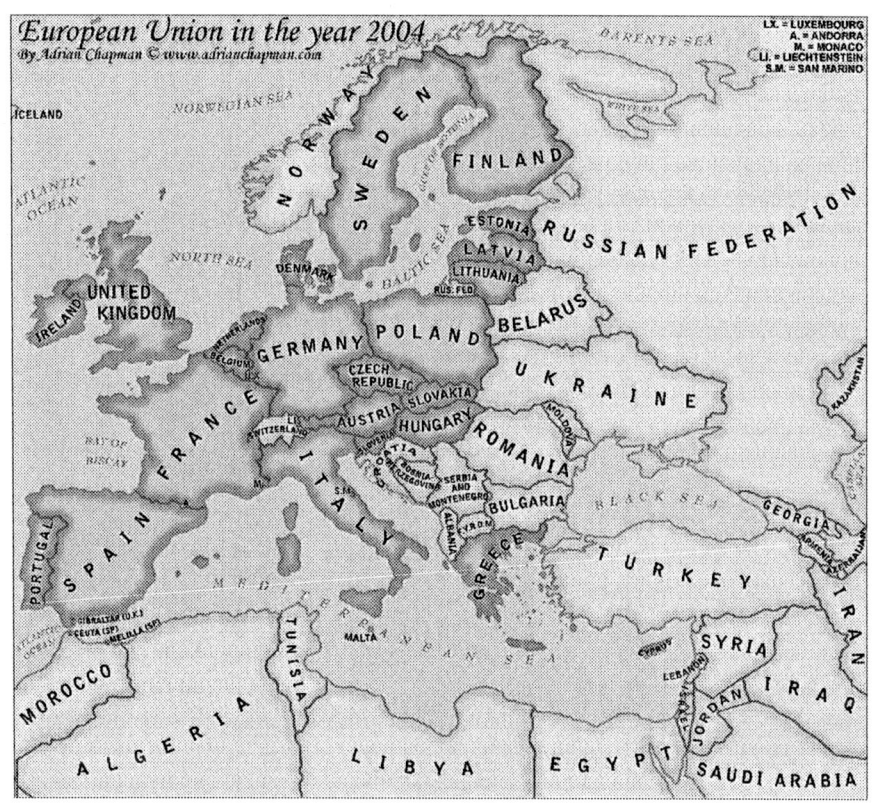

France

Just outside the town was the French Air Force aerodrome, Bron, with an old fort as its close neighbour. This fort was to be our accommodation for the next few weeks. It was little better than the camp in Romania, at least there I had a bed, whilst here I only had a straw palliasse on the floor. I suppose the French government had enough trouble finding quarters for their own freshly mobilised men plus their colonial troops without having to put up hordes of unexpected visitors. Local tailors were organised to produce a few thousand uniforms and gradually we re-acquired the appearance of a disciplined military force. There was no urgency about anything.

We were supposed to familiarise ourselves with French aircraft and their operation and maintenance. On some days I had access to a Potez 631 to study its construction, function of controls and instrument panel, but without a manual or anybody to explain anything it was a rather disheartening task. I found the afternoons particularly unproductive, due in part to the French custom that required bottles of "vin ordinaire" should be on the lunch table. Before we landed at Marseilles we had been briefed by our more experienced friends that a stay in France, the country of "le vin et l'amour" would be a pleasurable experience. The trouble was, that I for one, having been a teetotaller for most of my life, found that one glass of this "vin ordinaire" with lunch compelled me to have at least a half-an-hour's nap. This was not difficult to accomplish because for at least an hour after the meal a surprising peace reigned over the whole aerodrome. All I had to do was to murmur to my Sergeant Mechanic that I wanted to study the instrument panel of a particular Potez parked well away. I would go there and scramble into the pilot's cabin, take a lazy, bleary-eyed look round the fast-fading instrument panel and a few seconds later I was sound asleep. Whether I had any interesting dreams, I cannot remember. But one particular dream that pestered me frequently was that of a cat trying to settle on my lap. What was actually happening was that the control stick was bouncing between my legs. This was because the aerodrome was returning to life and my friend, the Sergeant, was "testing the ailerons" to make the control stick move right and left.

After a few weeks of "residing" in the fort, the conditions improved to the extent that we received some of our pay and also permission to live out. The majority of officers decided to look for a hotel or a boarding house within their means. Hrynasz and I were lucky to find a third rate hotel run by a Polish emigrant. Not only did we have to share the room but also a bed, of admittedly generous double-size dimensions. However, after all the nights in damp dungeons on palliasses we were ready to sleep four to such a bed! Breakfast was in the hotel but evening meals had to be found outside and this was how I learned my next sentence in French: "Patron! Jambon avec cornichon s'il vous plait". This simple meal of a slice of ham with a gherkin and a chunk of crisp bread was all we could afford until we started receiving our full pay. So our life was settling down to a routine of nights in the hotel, morning tram to Bron aerodrome, pottering about all day and coming back to the hotel and then for the "jambon avec cornichon" treat. Free time was spent exploring the city and learning French. Lyon is picturesquely situated on the confluence of the rivers Saone and Rhone and the town's three parts are connected by countless bridges.

Hrynasz had some schoolboy French, so his progress was good

and this made me rely on him to the detriment of my own progress in the French language. When looking for a suitable textbook I spotted "L'anglais sans peine". I still don't know why but something prompted me to buy this book and I did so there and then. I did not know enough French to use a French textbook for learning the English language but just the same I felt I had to try. It certainly was not easy and I might have given up but again luck or providence directed me to find an English teacher. I cannot recall how I managed this, possibly through the bookshop. So twice a week, for about three months, I had to cross two bridges and then go up by funicular railway to reach the western part of the city situated high above the river. As well as learning the language I was also learning about English customs and their way of life. My teacher was a calm and graceful lady, very patient and always encouraging. Occasionally the logic between the spelling and the pronunciation would lead me to despair and she would offer me a cup of tea - strong tea with milk! Babies in Poland were sometimes given weak tea with milk but this tea was more like tea essence. It was strong enough to make at least six cups of our *proper* tea with lemon. I found the English tea refreshing when thirsty but otherwise I had my reservations.

It was difficult to remember that the war was still on so the news on 10th May came as a shattering blow:

"GERMANS INVADING THE NETHERLANDS!!"

Next followed the conquest of Belgium and then, to our horror, the Maginot line failed to stop the flood of Panzers and the Wehrmacht pouring into north-eastern France. Our aerodrome was bombed repeatedly - sometimes we had an air raid warning but more often than not there was no warning at all.

There were trenches dug for diving in if caught unawares but I dreaded the thought of being half buried even before the bombs started falling. What really put me off the trenches was the effect of one such air raid. On that occasion I, with others, were near enough to the fort to run for shelter in there. After the air raid we walked out of the fort to the sight of the airfield buildings on fire, many aircraft destroyed and quite a few casualties. One of the trenches had received a direct hit and the bodies of those caught in it were literally shredded to pieces and scattered on the nearby road, grass and bushes. On one of the bushes I saw a scrap of human tissue hanging from a branch with something that looked like two eyeballs. Urrrgh!

After that whenever I could I would dash out into the nearby fields and trust my luck. I was not the only one with such an idea.

A few days later we had a particularly nasty and prolonged air raid, for which many of us ran out into our favourite field "shelter". After the "All Clear" signal we were heading back to the base. A couple of us were approaching the gate where we had to stand aside to let a car drive out. We could see the rank of Colonel on the cap of the officer in it so we saluted smartly and turned to go through the gate but before we had made a couple of steps there was a sudden screech of tyres due to hard braking and someone shouted:

"Lieutenants! The Colonel wants to see you!"

Our automatic reaction was to check all tunic buttons, square our caps up and check our ties. I found my top left breast pocket undone. This was quickly put right and we marched up to the car. We saluted and stood to attention only to be met by a tirade of scolding for "indiscipline and for being improperly dressed". The man was obviously in a state of shock after the raid but a Second Lieutenant does not point that out to a Colonel. Our names were noted with the order to report to the senior officer on duty the next day.

The next morning I went to the office where I found Major

Buczma on duty. I sighed with relief because I knew him as a tough but reasonable man, far removed from the apes of the Prussian style discipline. The Colonel's report was already on his desk and the Major was obviously embarrassed by it all. Apparently this Colonel had noticed my undone button and directed that I should be put on a charge and threatened with a few days in the military prison. Major Buczma did not elaborate but suggested that I see the Colonel the next day and try to apologise or explain. I could not see what there was to explain and was not in a hurry to face the "mad Colonel" in case I made things worse for myself. I decided to give it a couple of days and wait for a direct order to report. Needless to say my blood was up, not least because, according to some internal gossip, he was the officer who had shot a taxi driver in Warsaw for allegedly "insulting the honour of the uniform!" The trouble was that, according to some reporters, "one" of them was drunk! Well, I was going to keep out of his way for as long as I could. Next morning's air raid was earlier than usual. When we arrived at the base the first thing I saw was that the guardroom, containing the military jail, had been completely demolished! Was the Luftwaffe looking after me?

The same night I started feeling unwell. I blamed the "jambon avec cornichon" but Hrynasz, who had the same supper, was as fit as a cricket. I was sick all night and in the morning Hrynasz sent for a doctor from the base who took one look at me and declared:

"Hospital for you! You've got jaundice. Look at your finger nails".

I looked and instead of the usual pinky-white I saw yellow! My hands had a strange yellow tint and when I looked in the mirror I found the whites of my eyeballs far from white! So on May 16th I was admitted to a hospital in a town north of Lyon - I think it was Neuville. Strict diet and daily temperature measurement (using the peculiarly French method) rather spoilt the restful stay. When I could I tried to read the newspapers. The parts I could not understand were amply explained by the faces of my ward companions and nurses with frequent comments starting with: "Oh la la! Le Bosch this..!" and "Le Bosch that..!"

After two weeks I was sent "home" but was not quite cured – I still could not eat much and had continuous nausea. My skin was as yellow as ever. A few days later the doctor put me into another hospital - this time in Lyon where I shared a small room with another Polish Air Force officer. We were both rather worried because the war news was not good at all. It was getting worse day by day. We continued to study the papers and tried to get information from the staff but they were too busy with casualties coming from the front. We felt like a couple of frauds compared with the wounded. The headlines of June 15th made us both jump out of our beds:

"Paris has fallen! Germans marching under the Arc de Triumph!"

...and there we were, confined to beds!

The next day we had a visitor from our own unit who quite calmly informed us that the following day, 17th June, all Polish units stationed in Lyon were to assemble at the railway station to be evacuated further south. Apparently General Sikorski, who was then with the Polish Government in London, broadcast instructions to all Polish troops in France to make for ports on the Atlantic coast from Brest to St-Jean-de-Luz. These instructions were almost immediately amended - obviously for the benefit of units like ours in Lyon, which was too far south-east. Our instructions were to aim for one of the Mediterranean ports like Port-Vendres.

At once we asked the Sister in charge of our little ward to make arrangements for our instant discharge. She told us that we had to wait until the doctor had seen us and he was very busy. We waited the rest of the day and hardly slept at all that night - at first thinking how to solve our problem, then discussing various ideas of how to disappear from the hospital. Finally, we crept about as quietly as possible, assembling and packing our belongings. At breakfast we managed to keep very calm so as not to raise any suspicions but under our beds our cases were ready.

As soon as the nurses left us we put on our uniforms, picked up our cases and sneaked out towards the back staircase. Somebody did shout something after us but we had no inclination to hear or understand what it was all about. We took a tram to our lodgings, packed the rest of our possessions and caught another tram to the station. The train was already at the platform and most of our men were on board. Zygmunt saw me from his compartment and called me to join them. Almost collapsing with weakness and exhaustion, I was seated amongst my friends at last.

"Where are we going?" "South...probably Marseilles" was the answer.

Here we go again! We had no illusions that down south an attempt would be made to organise a line of resistance having seen many "Poilus" and Senegalese and other colonial troops retreating with only a few of them carrying rifles slung across their shoulders. So for many of us the 17th June was very much like the 2nd week of September of the previous year - in a different country and carried on a train but this time I had no responsibility for anybody except for myself.

In two days we had travelled only 300km and disembarked for one night at La-Cavalerie. The next two days took us as far as Port Vendres. It had taken four days to travel approximately 600km - about 400 miles! From Port Vendres railway station we had to march a few kilometres carrying all of our luggage. My arms and shoulders felt much worse than just tired by the time we reached our destination. This time our billets were almost on the beach of the Mediterranean Sea.

The position of our camp looked promising with a small port only a few kilometres to the north and the Spanish border not much further to the south. Not that we could expect a very friendly reception from the Spanish Government - most probably a march to an internment camp but with a much more Nazi-like atmosphere than that of the Romanian camp.

Our camp consisted of huts with just a layer of straw along their walls. The weather was warm and dry so this would not be too bad for a night or two but we had no idea how long we would have to stay there. Other questions churned in our minds: "Why so near the Spanish border? France has capitulated, but on what terms? Shall we be used as bargaining counters in exchange for the French soldiers in German hands?" These were not soothing thoughts. Then someone heard General Sikorski, our leader, speaking on the radio from London, with the news that England would welcome all Polish troops and again urging us to reach the nearest ports and make contact with British vessels. This news made us feel much better and we were confident that our senior officers would act on this advice as quickly as our present situation permitted. They had to be very diplomatic when dealing with the local French authorities. The bitterness, resulting from a rather swift defeat after all these slogans eg: "Ill ne passer pa parsque nous sons plus fort..., etc." hung over us like a threatening fog. Later on we heard that one of our units, which tried to reach Bordeaux, was stopped by the French forces and placed under arrest! Fortunately the camp was guarded by Senegalese troops who had better ideas how to treat their allies who had tried to stop the invaders.

We were prepared to settle down in the huts, but first let's have a bath in the sea. With soap in our hands we ran into the lazy waves of the Med. to have a good scrub. Having lived many miles away from salt water we did not realise that our soap would be quite ineffective. What disappointment and trouble for those who had started soaping their hair! Still, a good splash in salt water refreshed us enough to run back to the camp to finish ablutions under the tap.

After supper we pummelled the straw into something resembling a low couch, wrapped ourselves in blankets and tried to go to sleep. Sleep?? - not if the little beasts sharing our beds could help it. The warmth of our bodies must have brought whole armies of fleas to the surface. There was scratching and slapping and cursing everywhere. One joker was even keeping a score of kills and for a while there was keen competition and merriment. Then some one drew our attention to a double height heap of straw, which was not under the walls like ours, but completely separate at the end of the passage. White sheets were visible under the blankets and a pillow! A real pillow! Being the end of June it was still quite light and it was obvious that the owner of this catafalque-shape bed was not in yet. A quick conspiratorial, whispered conference and a few of us caught our tormentors instead of killing them and imprisoned them in a matchbox. Soon the box was simply hissing with their little legs scratching about trying to get out.

The silly little beasts could not understand why we suddenly gave up the chase and slaughter. A sentry posted at the door signalled that nobody was approaching so the owner of the matchbox, or the "flea internment camp", slipped it in between the sheets with the lid fully off. A couple of minutes later he pulled the box out. We hardly had time to resume our sleeping postures when the owner of the "super-bed" returned from ablutions. Fine pyjamas and a superior glance at the two rows of bodies under the walls made our anticipation even sweeter. I nearly shouted out "Whoopee!!" as I recognised the Colonel who tried to put me in jail and, I was convinced, caused my jaundice.

We had to pretend we were all asleep. And, as if to help us, the little biting blighters either from saturation or in disgust reduced their attacks on our skin to a bare minimum. Our victim in the meantime arranged his case as a bedside table, put his oddments on it and with a sigh of satisfaction slid in between the sheets. For a while there was peace on the "super-bed". Then a little jerk...next a hand scratching a leg...then another jerk. Then both hands busy! Turning over, both legs kicking out. Then all hell let loose!! Swearing in cavalry fashion (I thought he was not a true blood flyer!), he threw off the blankets, jumped out and began slapping himself all over. Finally, taking his pyjamas off, he dashed to the nearest window and started methodically hunting for his tormentors from head to foot and through his night attire and throwing them out.

This quite noisy activity provoked shouts from various directions:

"Quiet! we want to sleep!"...while the conspirators were killing themselves with laughter under the blankets. Whether he ever guessed that this was not an accidental concentration of the bloodthirsty insects I do not know. If he noticed that our supposedly sleeping forms were restless he would probably put it down to similar but milder attacks and not to laughter.

We woke up to the day in which France accepted the terms of surrender. "What terms? How does it affect us??" - were the worrying questions. Should we take matters into our own hands and cross the border into Spain? To what kind of reception?" After all, the political system there was similar to that in Germany and we could not expect them to help us to reach England. These questions were harassing our minds.

At the same time, similar but of a much higher importance, problems must have been discussed between the Polish representatives and those in France who wanted to continue the war against Hitler from the French bases in Algeria. On the 23rd June orders were issued for the immediate evacuation of the camp. I do not suppose that anybody could have done it faster than our group of the "globetrotters". Within minutes we were marching into the town where we were mustered on the quay facing a good-looking ship. A while later embarkation began.

The scene of this particular episode comes clearly to my mind every time I see my old briefcase, which I had purchased with my first salary after being commissioned. I had carefully guarded and carried it with me all the way from Krakow. All these thousands of miles and I nearly lost it here! To reach the deck of the ship we had to proceed up what looked like a plank of wood swinging on some ropes at the side of the ship. One had to concentrate on retaining balance and at the same time to hang on to one's possessions. Trying to get hold of a rope acting as a kind of a hand rail I happened to let the briefcase slip out of my hand and to my horror had to watch helplessly as it plunged into the strip of water between the quay and the ship. I must have yelled out something, probably a swear word, because almost instantly one of the sailors watching us from the quay grabbed a long pole with a hook on it and very expertly fished the case out as it came to the surface. Being filled with light things and containing a lot of air it was not in a hurry to sink to the bottom. Was I pleased?...and immensely grateful to that quick-acting sailor. Eventually I joined my group and was sent together with Zyg to share a twin-bunk cabin.

What a difference - we recalled our voyage from Romania to Malta. We went on deck to watch preparations to leave and to wave "goodbye" to France.

To our surprise there was no sign of the usual noise and bustle and throbbing of engines. After standing at the rails for a good while all we observed was a group of men in a heated discussion. One of them was our Senior Officer, the other the ship's Captain, both arguing with a French civilian and a gendarme. We wished we could hear what was going on but they were too far down on the quay. Whatever it was it did not make our Senior Officer happy. The French official's uncompromising attitude was expressive enough to fill us with foreboding. We spent the rest of the day and night tied up at the moorings.

I am still not quite sure what happened next but by later accounts the attitude of the local authorities was somehow reported to a unit of the Royal Navy which 'just happened to be near'. I cannot vouch to what extent it is true but the French Mayor was told to make up his mind and either let us go peacefully and "toute de suite", or to see his "Maison de Ville" and the nearby gendarmerie undergo some "structural alterations." The guns were surveying the little town menacingly and, needless to say, by breakfast time we were sailing away.

Africa and the Atlantic

This time the sea crossing was like a holiday trip: comfortable cabin, good food and a calm sea. We were settling down to a few days of restful voyage via Gibraltar to England hoping to have plenty of rest, sunbathing, and bridge parties. On the second day we expected to see a change of the ship's course to almost due west but to our surprise it was still almost due south, towards Africa obviously. This, of course, stirred up a new wave of speculations and enquiries, with the result that we were officially informed about negotiations between General Sikorski and the British Prime Minister regarding formation of Polish Forces on British soil. Our destination was England, but via Oran and Casablanca. These places were just names on the map to almost all of us. I never dreamt that I would ever have the opportunity to see the Mediterranean, and here I was crossing it to Africa! On Tuesday, 25th of June we landed in Algeria at the port of Oran.

WE ARE IN AFRICA!

Here was our once-in-a-lifetime chance to have a good look at this corner of the Black Continent. Our joy would be boundless if we could see the Atlas Mountains and sink our feet in the Saharan sands - even for just a few minutes. No such luck! We did not get a chance even to have a look at the town of Oran as we were marched from the ship straight to the waiting train, which took us to Sidi Chami for the night. We had to be satisfied with just relishing such a romantic name as Sidi Chami on our lips. To our thorough disgust we found that our night quarters were in a school denuded of all its furniture, not that the school desks would have been any more comfortable to sleep on than the bare floor.

Next morning, stiff and sleepy, we again embarked on the train and moved off towards Morocco. After travelling about 200 km and crossing the border between Algeria and Morocco we disembarked at Oujda for another rather uncomfortable night. The following day took us as far as Meknes where we were obviously expected. On the platform stood a seemingly endless line of benches and tables with plates, mugs, cutlery etc. A French officer and an N.C.O., in their colonial uniforms, invited us to a good meal. This was a great change after two days of rather nondescript snacks. Our quarters for the night were in the town and since we had a few hours to spare most of us went out to use what was for us an unique opportunity to see just a little of the Arab World. Everything looked like a film: the dazzling white buildings, the mosques, the street tradesmen, (we were warned never to pay the asking price), the women with their faces behind the yashmaks, real palm trees, fascinating narrow streets, public water pumps, and so on. Our eyes were very busy recording all these sights on our memory film tape. Saturated with such new impressions we went to bed to have a very comfortable night.

After another hot day on the train we finally reached Casablanca. We did not see much of this city because we arrived quite late in the evening, and the next morning we were marched straight to the harbour to embark. Crowded and not at all comfortable we set off for Gibraltar where, judging by our first contact with the Royal Navy, the conditions were sure to improve. Hugging the coast of Africa all day, we reached our destination. Sure enough, our hopes were visibly materialising, as gangways to another ship were opened and we crossed over full of expectation. We found ourselves in a hulk, which must have been used for transporting coal, there was black dust everywhere. Arrangements for sleeping and hygiene were very primitive.

There were many ships around us and we were eyeing with envy some smart looking passenger liners aboard which were people in uniforms and quite a few civilians. By next morning we were thoroughly disgusted with our bad luck but at about noon, we were told to prepare for yet another transfer. Surely conditions could only improve. We were not to be disappointed - the new ship had definitely been adapted for transporting troops.

There were very few cabins. Instead, each deck was like a large hangar with tables and benches from one end to another and with the space above them festooned with hundreds of hammocks at various levels. With a great deal of hilarity some of us started trying out our swinging beds. Not so bad at the lower level, but for the higher hammocks one had to be an acrobat to get in without immediately spilling out! Just as well we had the first night in the harbour - to get some practice of "going to bed" and to catch up with some sleep after that coal-bunker night.

The beginning of July found us still in Gibraltar harbour where we witnessed the partly-successful arrival of a group of French flyers who had escaped from France. "Partly"- because they arrived in a large four-engined aircraft with undercarriage but...it had to land on the water in the bay. The aircraft ploughed the water for a few hundred yards then settled down, and started sinking quite rapidly. All the Frenchmen were saved.

On 2nd July at about noon, our ship and all the ships in our vicinity, suddenly came to life. Smoke appeared from stacks and the rumbling of engines could be heard everywhere. After some manoeuvring we found ourselves in a convoy of about two dozen ships of all shapes and sizes sailing slowly round "the Rock" and out into the open sea. A number of Navy Units appeared, taking positions to protect us from all directions and all together we were moving rather slowly out into the Atlantic. Our progress was slow because we had some ships that were unable to keep up with the more modern vessels. While the ships were organised into a convoy we were lined up on deck, issued with lifejackets and instructed on procedure in case of emergency. We knew very well that "emergency" meant torpedo attack from a German U-boat. Next we were divided into groups and allocated lifeboats, with a severe warning that these boats were not to be used as bedrooms however tempting that might be!

The weather was kind to us, so after a restful day spent mostly on deck, we went below for the night. The performance with the hammocks was repeated, only this time the motion of the ship complicated our acrobatics to the extent that general hilarity was punctuated with some swearing and even yelps of pain caused by crashing down to the deck. The night was hot and after a few hours the air was getting rather thick - we had been told to keep the portholes closed. I do not think that I slept more than a few hours. As soon as I could see some daylight I climbed out of my hammock and crept out for some fresh air on the top deck. Zyg was already there, gazing sadly towards the east. Did he want to see the sunrise or was his mind a few more thousand miles in that direction, visualising the situation in Poland during recent months? We did not talk, just stood side by side looking at the wake of our ship and the dark silhouettes of the rest of the convoy against the pink sky. Just gazing, without registering what was visible to our eyes but reliving the scenes from our very recent life: France, Romania and Poland. What's happened to my family?! My brother in the army?!!

A shout - "Come down! - Breakfast!" brought our minds back to the ship. "Time for breakfast" meant that all hammocks had to be rolled up and the sleeping hall converted into a breakfast room. Portholes were opened and the fresh air whistling through pushed the foul air out over the Atlantic. By now we were getting used to the milky soup with some kind of flakes in it and, new to us, a kind of confiture served on a plate for each table. The first time this plate with orange confiture (which I now know as marmalade and quite like it) was placed on our table, one of our group sitting at that point thought it was his second course and without more ado started eating it. At the second mouthful he pulled a long face and stopped eating!

A similar, funny incident occurred at lunch when the main course was served on one large soup plate full of bits of cauliflower, onion, beans and slices of cucumber, all drowning in some yellow sauce. It landed in front of our "marmalade expert" since he was sitting at that end of the table. He carefully lifted some of it on the tip of his fork, tasted it, pulled a horrible face and immediately passed the plate on. This process was repeated by almost everybody until the last man sitting by the open porthole simply scraped the contents out into the sea to a general laughter of agreement. The kitchen staff, seeing the plate scraped clean, of what I now know as Piccalilli, assumed that "Those Poles love this highly spiced stuff". So for our next day's lunch the plate was not just filled but heaped with it. This could have gone on for days had the weather not deteriorated, forcing us to keep the portholes closed. I suppose that the sudden change in our taste might have been explained by the choppy seas but why was the rest of the menu not returned?

When bedtime was approaching I decided that the air in our dining/bedroom would be unbearable, so I rolled up my blankets, picked up the life belt and my small case of essentials, and went up on deck. The cosiest corners were already occupied. Looking round I spotted someone sitting by the shaft of the spare anchor and arranging his blankets. The other side was free so I claimed it as my "bedroom" - and who was on the other side? No one else but Zygmunt again! We chatted for a while looking at the stars and were soon fast asleep. That was when I discovered that a life belt folded and covered with a towel made quite a passable pillow.

The great armada of ships kept on going and the escort units were weaving their intricate pattern protecting us all the time. On Saturday the sea became rough and by Sunday we had quite a gale. The convoy did not look so orderly any more. The smaller vessels were often not visible behind huge waves. Suddenly, there was a noticeable change of stations in the rear part of the convoy. Apparently what happened was that a small ship, which most probably had never before left the coastal waters, found the Atlantic breakers too high, and capsized. One destroyer stayed with it to rescue as many as possible under these circumstances. What impressed us was the discipline of the convoy, which sailed on as if nothing had happened.

By nightfall we were not sure whether to stay in our "anchor bedrooms" with the spray often flying right over our heads, but in the end decided to risk getting wet rather than being suffocated below deck. It was not too bad, although we found it difficult to get to sleep. Talking against the noise of the wind and sea was almost impossible, until suddenly Zyg shouted, "Look up!" The sky was clear and we could see the stars with the pole star straight ahead of us! For the last four nights it had been firmly on our right; now it had moved to the front - so we were sailing north! After four days and nights of sailing west we were becoming convinced that there must have been a change of orders and we were on our way to Canada - or maybe America? America was not at war, so we reasoned that it must be Canada. This change of course put an end to our speculations and we realised that the prolonged manoeuvre was necessary to avoid the U-boats. By now we must have been half way across the ocean. During the following night our guiding star shifted to our left and at the same time clouds appeared. The weather gradually deteriorated and it started to rain so we decided to give up our "holiday" on deck, and return to our hammocks.

After breakfast on 12th of July I went "upstairs" and immediately noticed some of my pals excitedly pointing to our right - "Land!!", I could hear them shouting.

"Look, over there, slightly behind the ships!"

This must be England was the general conclusion. In the afternoon the land became quite clearly visible in front of us. Soon the deck was crowded with everybody trying to see England - for us, the "Promised Land". Before long we could see tall buildings, chimneys and cranes. We were ordered to get ready to disembark. Everybody was so excited about reaching our destination that this did not take long at all.

We are in England! (Learning English)

Within an hour our group of junior officers not only left the ship but marched to a nearby railway station and got on the train. There were a couple of hundred aircrew plus aircraft engineers, admin-staff and, of course, half a dozen Senior Officers. Half an hour later the train started, and only then we realised that in all that excitement we had missed our lunch! But here was our first example of the perfect organisation of handling the transportation of quite a large group of soldiers. A message was passed down to each coach to send four volunteers to the first wagon to collect food and drink for their coach. It was not a full meal, but enough to "keep us going", with the promise of a better 'do' upon arrival.

It was getting dark when the train stopped. We were ordered to put our luggage, which consisted mainly of a haversack and a small case, on a lorry, form marching columns and set off to our camp. We left the town and about half an hour later stopped at a gate beyond which we could see a square with rows of huts along two sides. In the middle of the square the lorry with our luggage was waiting for us. Allocation to the huts was quick. As we were collecting our luggage we were told to assemble in 20 minutes in the "Mess" - which we were told was the building along the third side of the square. We found out that the "Mess" was a restaurant with an evening meal for us. After the meal we were told to get to bed before 10.00 o'clock, with a promise of reveille at 6.00 o'clock and breakfast at 7.30 after some physical exercises. SO!...it was back to the days of the Military College!

6.00 o'clock arrived much too soon; we could have done with 12 hours sleep after all those days at sea but at least we had the chance of a good shower and decent shave after a long run, as our morning exercise. Then breakfast....and then what? We expected some kind of briefing about formation of squadrons, retraining and familiarisation with new equipment and so on. What we got was the most thorough and prolonged medical parade! We were checked meticulously from feet to scalp - it took all day! A very sensible precaution; after all it was at least eleven months since most of us had been anywhere near proper medical care, and during that long time we experienced some extreme conditions of hygiene and dubious food or companions, for example, the "red light districts of entertainment" in France. Most of us enjoined the visits to such "maison" but the unlucky ones brought with them some nasty "souvenirs".

The next day most of us started the so-called "square bashing", whilst some had to undergo another medical inspection. This produced comments on the lines of "Countries on the Continent are being invaded one after another. Hitler's menacing war machine is breathing its foul breath across the Channel, and here we are wasting time on medical parades and square bashing! Really!!" However, "Orders are Orders", so we had to settle down to this unexpected routine. It had its comical turns since our instructors were English N.C.O.s. These chaps must have had nerves of steel! We did not understand, at first, what was the meaning of a command sounding like, "SHUN!" or "ANDADEEZ". As to formation in three lines - that was completely new to us. Our formation was in two lines, which, in one swift manoeuvre, became a column of four rows ready for marching away. The comical situations occurred when those who quickly picked up the meaning of such commands, did what was expected and the others, who did not understand, hesitated or did nothing. I must admit that some of us played this game for longer than the language puzzles really warranted; the feeling of frustration was growing under the superficial fun. "Here we are marching about, listening to lectures for hours and in general behaving like a large jamboree of grown up scouts with nothing better to do." Years later I became convinced that again we were unknowingly experiencing another example of thorough, un-panicked planning. Surely we had to be given a chance to cool off after the last few weeks of stress and discomfort although it is amazing how young men in groups, with an important mission, can take it and make light of it. Also, I would not be surprised at all if the English authorities wanted to observe us for a while and assess the real value of our impatience to get armed and have a bash at the enemy.

A couple of weeks later we had to face tailors who took the essential measurements for our new uniforms. Before long we received the uniforms of the Royal Air Force with a small label on the shoulders stating "POLAND". By now our instruction sessions included English. Very few of us had any English from school as the usual choice in Polish schools was French or German. Latin and Greek were compulsory in my school and since I had opted for German I had some knowledge of the three most useful languages for learning English. Many English words are similar to German, eg: bread and butter = "brot und butter". The more complicated scientific and medical words are based on the classic languages. With this kind of background some of us had an advantage, so as soon as we could manage a few phrases in English we were keen to try them out in the shops, on the buses etc. Our attempts were very kindly received by the locals, who patiently listened to our appalling pronunciation and our stammering from one wrong word to another.

To our utter astonishment, only about three weeks after landing in this country, we were invited to a local school concert (on August 5th) to perform on stage entertaining the audience with a vocal number. It so happened that four of us, Rysiek, "Wutur", Ostach and myself had been performing as a "Revellers Group" whilst at the College in Warsaw. This was a group of singers where Rysiek sang as well as played the piano for accompaniment; but there was no screeching or moaning, no chewing of microphones, no peculiar hairdo and as for the "fancy" dress - we had to wear our uniforms!

Four days later our complete group was transferred to Blackpool to join a few hundred Air Force men coming from other camps. I believe that this was as a result of some new Anglo-Polish agreement, which was the basis of formation of Polish Armed Forces in England. We were allowed to have the Polish Eagle on our caps and at last the "square bashing" reverted to the old familiar form. The Blackpool inhabitants and holidaymakers must have had a shock when we practised our review march, which is a gentler form of the notorious "goose-stepping". Our quarters were in hotels throughout Blackpool, allocation to which was achieved by reading our names from an alphabetical list. So ten of us with names beginning with the letter "S" were sent to the Hartford Hotel. The hotel owner, an elderly gentleman, received us with a high degree of trepidation. He had only recently retired from some onerous job and had bought the hotel with the idea of gentle, part-time supervision of staff from his office. When the war broke out most of his staff were called up to the armed forces or to some other form of the war effort. To make matters worse for him, during the last few months he had had to accommodate a group of pregnant women evacuated from Manchester. Now he had to accept ten foreigners full of "joie de vivre", speaking very little English and eyeing up any of his precious female guests between 18 and 40 years old! There happened to be an elderly couple who immediately captivated the hearts of most of us by their almost parental interest in all our activities. Mr and Mrs Willson even gave us an open invitation to visit them for a cup of tea sometime - only two of us managed to accomplish this, many months later.

Of course, the purpose of our presence in a holiday resort was not to have a good time, but to attend a very intensive course in English and lectures on the King's Regulations...quite apart from the physical exercises and drill. For our spare time there were cinemas, beaches, Blackpool Tower and card games.

Two young men who were teachers, were also staying in this hotel. They had been requested by their Education Authority to spend their holiday within easy reach of their schools. One of them, quite unwittingly, became the hand of fate in my life (five years later). My friend Julian and myself became friendly with the two teachers: Jack and Vin. Jack Riley taught in Morecambe and Vin Newton in a village near Lancaster. Both of them had a wonderful sense of humour and must have had limitless patience when hearing not just our broken but simply shattered English. Before the end of their holiday they took us both to be introduced to their families who received us with a very warm welcome and soon afterwards we received an invitation to go with them for a day in the Lake District, an area they quite obviously loved. For us the Lakeland hills were rather tame after the Tatra Mountains and did not provide enough challenge for our youthful energy; but after a couple of visits the scenery became a kind of haunting melody - one wanted more and more of it.

Now, after many visits, every time I get within sight of the hills and lakes my soul floats peacefully over the gentle fells, hovers over each changing shade of green or races with the cloud shadows, swiftly climbing up to the top only to cascade down into the next valley. The thundering Aira or Skelwith Force or the shimmering and tinkling Yewdale Beck, have as much magnetic power as the tiny, gurgling stream under the Iron Bridge…but only when I am holding the hand of my beloved wife. Oh, Oh! Here I am almost giving away the secret that I want to keep for another five years.

Our first and unforgettable Christmas in England was in the homes of Jack and Vin. We were introduced to some hilarious games like "Charade" or "Murder." Vin's elderly Aunt would not take part in the "Murder" game for fear that "...these Polish Airmen might not understand that it is only a pretend murder!" - I only discovered this much later of course.

By now my English was shaping up quite well and I was transferred to a class with the grand name of "Trainee Interpreters". Soon after the New Year of 1941 I was asked to help those who were struggling and the newcomers still arriving from the distant corners of Europe. Here I have to express my deep gratitude to both Jack and Vin and their families for giving Julian and myself a tremendous boost in learning the language. They gave us the important chance to practice speaking it as well as hearing English spoken.

After Christmas a couple with a teenage girl arrived at the hotel. They must have had friends in the town because during the following days "our" resident girl had a visitor - another young lady. This, of course, attracted a lot of attention from our side which developed into smiles from both sides and then greetings, and somehow or other four of us were invited to a party by the local girl. They decided to have an evening tea and dance and our young hostess organised two more young ladies from her school. Between them they laid on a buffet; much more interesting than rations would allow, whilst we for our part, provided the drinks. The party was getting into a full swing, the buffet demolished, the floor cleared for dancing, and the record player was switched on. We stopped only for changing the records and for liquid refreshments. The company was getting noticeably "warmer", the dancing rather slow and dreamy, when suddenly the air-raid sirens shattered the romantic atmosphere - like the sound of the front door banging to signal the return of parents! The hostess started checking the windows for blackout. We suggested that she should put the lights out (Oh no! Oh no! The purpose was not at all what is in your mind!) and open the windows to listen out for the dreadful drone of the German bombers and to watch the display of searchlights and tracery of the ack-ack guns. Soon we could hear them approaching...but no searchlights, and no gun fire?! "Where are they going tonight? Have they missed Liverpool?" we were wondering. As if to answer our questions we heard a very thin whistle, which was well ingrained in our memories from Poland and France. What followed were just very surprisingly soft "flop, flop" sounds and no explosions.

In front of our windows was an open space, a park or a school playground where small flickering fires suddenly appeared here and there. "Incendiaries!?!" We knew that they were used mainly as target markers for the bombers, so our plan of action was obvious: "Put out as many as possible! And as fast as possible!" We all dashed out and started groping in the dark for the way into the field when we heard a crash on the roof. Two of us, together with the hostess, turned back. She showed us the way to the top while I grabbed a shovel from the fireplace and we scrambled up. The flaming thing was small so it did not penetrate the tiles but rolled down into the gutter. This, very fortunately, was accessible with only a small amount of acrobatics, so without looking where it would land I dislodged it and tipped it out into the back garden. The rest of our party was already very busy out in the field. We dashed down as fast as we could first of all to deal with our little "treasure." The garden soil was quite soft so it was easy to scoop it up and cover the "bomb". A good layer of soil would make the flames invisible and most likely put it out. This proved more difficult out in the field as being a rough meadow it needed a lot of effort to kick up and scoop enough of it to cover a few of these nasty things. In the excitement of running here and there and struggling to lift some soil we did not notice that the raid was over - no more droning engines above but neither was there an "all clear" siren. It must have been a lost navigator and a jittery bomb-aimer who were responsible for ruining our party. Luckily most of the incendiaries seemed to have landed within our reach and were made harmless, so with filthy hands and shoes we returned to tidy ourselves up and to say "Good Bye" to our young ladies.

At the end of February I got a posting to West Frough in Scotland as an interpreter in a gunnery school training Polish Air Gunners. They must have been desperately short of interpreters to appoint me! Trainee air gunners came and went. My work, at first quite interesting and occasionally exciting, gradually became routine and even boring. This kind of feeling must have been even worse for the pilots sent there partly to build up their flying experience and also to be pure and simple "bus drivers" for the trainees behind them. It was not at all surprising therefore, that after two or three months of towing the 'sleeve' for the air-to-air gunnery practice, such pilots were gripped by an irresistible urge to "freak out" - to do something more exciting. This, more often than not, consisted of "shooting up" a lake or a solitary tree in a field, which sometimes happened to be near a village. Such performances had nothing to do with guns or shooting - it simply involved a low level, high-speed swoop over a target and a quick getaway.

Today, in the era of the jet aircraft, this can be quite terrifying for those on the receiving end. Attack by an aircraft at almost the speed of sound gives one no warning whatsoever - just a sudden, deafening crash of thunder right over one's head: enough to make one miss a heartbeat or two! It is a cruel thing to do; but in 1941-42, especially flying the "Battle" aircraft, one could only attack at the speed of a third of that of sound, say at about 200 mph, which means that the sound would precede the aircraft by a mile or so. Just the same, when "hedge hopping" one could cause quite a scare and bewilderment if the "target" happened to be a peaceful village.

Well, one of these pilots very foolishly decided to impress the village by his skill of low level flying when he thundered the whole length of its high street. This was simply too much for the otherwise very patient Scots - somebody spotted the identification letters of the aircraft and reported it to the police. The Station Commander had the pilot in his office together with his Flight Commander, to investigate whether there was an excuse for such behaviour...training purposes say. There was none, so the pilot had to face a Court Martial. I was asked to interpret for him and the idea terrified me! Translating a lecture given in English to a group of Polish trainee air gunners is one thing but to translate the utterances of the accused in Court, accurately and without delay, in a completely new subject, was quite a different matter.

To illustrate the level of my English at that time - when one of my fellow officers asked me why it is called "Court Martial" I promptly informed him that it is because it is usually presided over by an "Air Marshal". I had not seen it written, and to me the sound of these two words had no other meaning...

To my immense relief the Air Marshal arrived with his adjutant and a Polish officer who obviously spoke perfect English. Anyway, the hapless N.C.O. was suspended from flying for a while and I believe, lost prospects of promotion for a period. The sentence was rather mild but the need for pilots, whether disciplined or over-enthusiastic, was too great and too urgent to do anything else.

I was glad to return to my normal translations, which I considered as rather important, because I was helping to train aircrews for Polish bombers and it was essential that these fellows knew their job well. Their lives and the lives of the whole crew would often be in their hands... as I was to find out later. After a few weeks of helping the English instructor, who tried to explain armament, tactics, procedures etc, all new subjects to me, I decided that the most effective way would be if I did the whole course in English myself.

My Air Gunnery "crash course" lasted 6-weeks. I was awarded the Gunners Wing, which I proudly accepted, but at the same time I strongly emphasised that I did not want to be anything other than a pilot. This was accepted by my superiors. There were many Polish pilots at this airfield who had only recently qualified on British aircraft and were gaining experience by flying the air-gunners or towing the 'sleeves' for the firing exercises. Sometimes they had to carry trainee navigators in practical tests of their theoretical knowledge. Some of them were my friends with whom I had taken the English course in Blackpool. They did not have to serve as interpreters for months and months but the lucky fellows went straight to the flying training stations. Occasionally I would be invited by one of them to join him in a "weather test" and I would be allowed to take over piloting, just to give me the taste of things to come.

First Steps in the Right Direction

In December 1941 the Japanese attacked Pearl Harbour and within days I received orders to report at the Flying Training School...in Torquay of all places. I knew that there was no airfield and no actual flying training done near that famous holiday resort. What I did not know, however, was that the British authorities would insist on giving us a thorough training regardless of the new developments.

So...back to hours of classroom work, learning the elements of navigation and signalling. This was interspersed with energetic physical training and some rather unusual games that were quite new to us. In such a game you would have to try to get hold of a football but as soon as you succeeded you would be attacked and most often thrown to the ground, sat upon, pushed and pulled until someone else would rip the ball out of your arms. This would not have been too cruel, however pointless, had the playing field been grass and not a hard (cement) tennis court! My suspicion was that it was a method of testing us for such qualities as tenacity, aggressiveness, quick reaction and indifference to pain when elbows were scraped raw on the cement.

One sunny morning our instruction was on signalling by means of an Aldis lamp. We were out in the open when the roar of aircraft and almost simultaneous explosions suddenly shattered the peace. I just could not believe it! Here, in a peaceful corner of Devon in a holiday resort just like in Blackpool, we were being attacked by the Luftwaffe once again! Surely there was nothing special about the little harbour. They missed it anyway and dropped the bombs on a large hotel that just happened to be convalescent home for aircrews.

Or....did they really miss their target??? The hotel was about a mile inland and the attack was low level...too low for error. I suspected that their recent reconnaissance flights had taken back photographs of men in uniform near the hotel. That they were on convalescence in wheelchairs or on deckchairs on the terrace, getting the benefit of the winter sunshine, was beyond the intelligence of people like Hermann Goering. A couple of hours later we learned that there had been a simultaneous attack on the harbour. It must have acted as a camouflage for the two bombers that would appear to have overshot their aim!

By the end of March 1942 we were deemed to have swallowed enough elementary theory required to be qualified for the next stage. After an examination we were given one week's leave with orders to report at RAF Hucknall near Nottingham after our little holiday.

A few very pleasant days with my adopted family in Lancaster were very welcome. So much further north and away from the French coast with its "hit and run" sneaky raiders I thought that we would be in absolute peace but no such luck. During my six-day visit there, I witnessed two merciless bombing raids on Barrow-in-Furness. The town and the shipyard were not visible to us because of distance and late evening but the horizon in that direction glowed red and was full of violent flashes. My host, Alan, was in the Lancaster Voluntary Fire Service and in an emergency his unit would be sent to help in Barrow. One could feel a great relief in the house when he appeared about an hour after the "all clear" sirens. These men often had to stay on duty until late at night and then had to go to work next day as usual!

The leave over, I reported to the Initial Flying Training School. This was at last something more to my liking...something to do with aeroplanes and flying, not classrooms and lectures. The aircraft were "Tiger Moths" - light biplanes and very good for beginners. By mid-April I had my first "dual" flight, which means flying with an instructor at the controls of the aircraft. I managed to score 2 hours and 40 minutes of flying 'dual' in only a couple of days. That was sufficient to be sent on my first solo flight - I could hardly contain my satisfaction or my excitement. Such apparently rapid progress was due to the thorough elementary flying training we had received whilst at the Cadet School in Warsaw before the war. In small measure it was also due to some air experience whilst on duty in Scotland.

Now I am going to attempt to paint the delights of flying. First I must humbly admit that my poetic vocabulary is completely inadequate to fully express the delights of flying. I wish I could convey to you the hammering of the heart, the soaring of the soul, the majesty of mountainous clouds, the poetry of the fields, woods, rivers and lakes at my feet...and above all the feeling of freedom and of the whole world belonging to me! This may be unbearably boring for some of you. On the other hand - those who have experienced similar sensations might like to live through them again and those of you who are at the stage of hoping to find out what it is like may find it encouraging not to give up dreaming. Also...doing all those tricks in a gentle creature like the Tiger Moth makes you appear like a strong breeze blowing over the countryside whilst in a jet aircraft you would be like a hurricane gone wild!

At this point I feel it only fair that to warn those readers who are not considering taking flying lessons or who are not sufficiently interested in reading pages of detailed instructions for carrying out certain manoeuvres in the air, to skip a few pages and start reading again on page 126.

The purpose of the second stage of flying training was to build up our complete self-confidence in control of the aircraft and to achieve the skill to perform the required manoeuvres very precisely. Aerobatics was something completely new to me. Whilst training in Poland we were allowed to do steep turns and gentle spins. An aircraft in a spin can be in danger and one had to learn to counteract that. As far as such stunts like looping-the-loop, a barrel or an "Immelmann" were concerned, I could only see them on film, or a little later, just before the war started, I could watch the fighter pilots in my squadron in Krakow filling the skies with mock fights accompanied by the roar of engines. I was then shown by my instructor how to perform these "beauties" and after a few repeats I was sent to do them by myself. These were wonderful hours.

First, laborious climbing to the maximum height the engines could manage...with ears "popping" due to changes in the air pressure and the engine roaring, one could reach about 15,000 feet. At that height the roads below become threads, the railway a straight and darker line and to the East, the bluish-grey ribbon of the River Trent. It was important to note these landmarks in relation to the position of the sun so that at the end of the performance one could very quickly determine one's position again in relation to the airfield. Of course, at the end your height would only be about 1500 feet and so the terrain would appear totally different. Anyway, before beginning, check that no other budding "stunt pilot" is performing in the vicinity and let the fun begin! A shallow dive to gather speed, gradually open the throttle, then pull the "stick" to the chest to get the "kite" into a vertical climb. The climb does not last very long with such a feeble engine so as the speed approaches the lower critical level push the rudder right out to achieve a gentle vertical about turn. Now I am diving vertically with the speedometer racing through 80, 100, 120 mph...and higher. Gently pull on the stick and in a smooth arc change from the dive to horizontal flight. Open the throttle to maintain full speed and still pulling on the stick change to vertical and with the engine at full revs gradually return to horizontal flight but in an inverted or upside down position. Reduce the throttle and complete the "loop" and then decide on the next figure.

When changing the path of flight from dive to horizontal and then upwards again the centrifugal force makes your body feel three or four times heavier and requires a conscious effort even to keep your jaw closed. Should you exceed the speed or reduce the radius of the circle too much you may find the day becoming dull, your vision difficult and even your brain not functioning as normal. There is a danger of fainting and losing control of the aircraft. If in the top of the circle in the upside down position your speed is too low you may feel weightless for a second or two, lose contact with the seat and even get suspended by the seat belts. All this had been explained and even partly experienced when flying with the instructor so I tried not to overdo the turn.

So the loop has been satisfactorily performed. Still high enough and with good speed - so how about a "slow barrel"? ie: a spin through 360° in horizontal flight. Have a go! Push the stick to the left and gradually push the right foot in all the way. Watch the horizon and the speed. The aircraft's nose should not leave the horizon when the left wing is gradually going down until vertically pointing towards the earth. Continue rotating into the inverted position. Maintain horizontal path with the help of the engine and pulling the right foot in. Still rotating, with the left wing going towards vertical push the left foot in and as the aircraft is returning to it's normal position gradually pull the left foot back again. I must add that it is much easier to perform this manoeuvre in a vertical dive or a high-speed vertical ascent when gravity is not interfering with your efforts.

By now there is not enough altitude left for anything else except one full 360° turn to the left and one to the right…again struggling to keep the "nose" on the horizon. Now level out and look for the base. The roads now look like wide ribbons with little model lorries slowly moving on them. The railway track is right below and Nottingham visible in front. So climb a little, do an about turn and follow the railway looking out for the aerodrome. After a couple of minutes it appears in front at "11 o'clock", which means slightly to the left. Keep a sharp lookout for other aircraft coming in to land or ready for take off. Not too busy right now so line up for landing and watch the control caravan on the edge of the field. Green light - final approach, losing altitude and speed - lower and lower and then wheels make contact with the field. Bearably smooth landing. "Taxi" towards the hangar to hand over the Tiger Moth to the mechanics. Report to the O.C. Flight, fill in the logbook and join the other "eaglets" to brag about the hair-raising stunts we have all performed.

There were also many hours of less exciting flying to be done, e.g. map-reading, simulated forced landing, etc. When practising instrument flying - with an instructor of course – I had a hood fixed right over me so that I could only see the instrument panel whilst the instructor could keep an eye on things and take over in an emergency.

Another kind of training was Link Trainer flying. This was done in a kind of a box, fully equipped with flying controls and instruments – a flight simulator as it is now called. The box itself was suspended on a number of pneumatic jacks which reacted to the flying controls so well that it created a quite realistic impression of actual flying except for the effects of acceleration and centrifugal forces. The instructor had the means of "changing the weather", he could produce the effect of the aircraft being damaged in a variety of manners, e.g. cut out the engine, make the flying controls less responsive, etc.

Low-level flying was much more interesting and exciting. At say, 300 feet, you get the full effect of speed with fields, hedges, trees and houses flashing by. But keep a sharp look out for power lines! The training program included a good deal of classroom lessons, learning regulations, airfield controls, emergency procedures etc.

By mid-June my group must have reached the required standard and as a result I found myself packing once again. From this point on our work was to be on a much more serious level. We had to move to an airfield not far away but of much more serious character. Here our future would be decided as some of us would be considered suitable for Bomber Command No.1 Training Squadron and some for Fighter Command No.2 Squadron. The decision would be based on a summary of reports from all stages of work and training.

The Station Commanding Officer made a brief welcoming speech, then handed us over to his adjutant who then read out a list of names for each squadron. I found myself in Squadron No.1 and was not sure whether to feel pleased or disappointed. The fighter pilots had all the glamour after the fighting in the Battle of Britain, especially our 303 Fighter Squadron but by now, in mid-1942, the bombers were in a serious large-scale offensive. The 1000 bomber raid on Cologne was still a hot topic but so was the fast increasing rate of losses. Anyway, somebody at H.Q. must have come to the conclusion that I had to be trained as a bomber pilot to speed up the day of victory, so that was that.

Squadron No.1 was equipped with Airspeed Oxfords – twin-engined aircraft with retractable undercarriage and even a radio. After the simple, slow, open cockpit biplanes this was like changing from running about on scooters to driving proper cars. First of all we had a few hours of familiarisation with the construction and controls of the new (to us) machine, then some words of wisdom from the experienced flyers of Oxfords about its idiosyncrasies and phobias. Finally, after about 11 hours of dual flying, I was sent on my first solo trip. Peculiar experience, sitting in a large cockpit with nobody else next to me…the second control kept moving about as if a ghost had its invisible hands on it. After a few solos I got used to the emptiness of the large body. The weather was wonderful so the grand total of flying hours climbed rapidly. The day came when I was taken for instrument flying (ie: when I could only see the instrument panel) while my instructor, sitting next to me had to be ready to take over in case my attempt of, say, blind landing on a subsidiary airfield was not safe enough. This was repeated over and over until the mystery of instrument flying and landing became much less of a mystery. With the longer nights in September we started actual operational night flying.

Now I could clearly see the necessity of so many hours of practice in instrument flying supported by the Link Trainer hours. On take-off after dark and as soon as the airfield lights disappeared behind us there was nothing to latch on to help me check the angle of climb and the lateral balance of my Oxford other than the instruments. One had to watch at least three gauges at once: speed, artificial horizon and compass. On my first take-off in spite of the instruments doing their best to make my effort look awful, we reached the required height and I was told to make a 90° left turn. Very gingerly I tilted the left wing down and concentrated on the compass, watching it going slowly through 220°, 210°, 200°, etc. What I failed to see was that the artificial horizon was showing greater and greater angle of tilt until I suddenly felt a jolt on the volant [steering wheel]. My instructor had had to correct the tilt to avoid a dangerous vertical slide. As soon as we got ourselves sorted out I was ordered to carry out another 90° turn, but better this time. So I started again with my eyes darting from the compass to the Artificial Horizon and at the same time listening to the sound of the engines for any change in revs. A steady drone was the indication that we were not beginning to slide down. The turn this time was much smoother.

By now we found ourselves progressing down wind and parallel to the flare path which indicated the position of the runway. I had time to admire the slowly moving procession of lights with a flashing light at the far end and mini-lights of another night flier corning in to land. After a couple of minutes, well beyond the runway, I had to do two 90° turns to line up with the parallel lights of the flare path. My heart began beating faster because I was approaching the moment which requires a high precision in angle of descent, speed and direction. When approaching to land a pilot can see two sets of coloured lights marking the beginning of the runway - just like traffic lights. He can also see two long lines of lights, one on each side of the landing path known as the "flare path". The "traffic lights" are projected at an angle to the horizontal with the orange taking the top part, green the middle part and red the bottom part of the arc. This helps the pilot to make the approach at the correct angle of descent into the green light zone - coming into the red would be too low and dangerous. This system can be refined by slightly raising the lights on the left side of the beginning of the runway so that in the best angle of approach one can see green on the left and orange light on the right side.

The throttles had to be adjusted...but very gently. Less...less gas. The flare path appeared to be almost on the level with us.

Coloured lights flashed past...gas reduced further, pilot pulls the volant more and more...the aircraft loses almost all buoyancy and bounces when the wheels touch the tarmac with a screech. After another moment afloat, contact with the runway is made again and this time throttles are closed and rolling begins with speed gradually decreasing to only a few m.p.h. "Phew - it was quite good, wasn't it?" I asked myself but did I do it all myself or was the hand of my experienced instructor, F.O. Krasnik, on the controls more firmly than I realised?

My self-congratulations were rudely interrupted by an order to taxi round back to the starting point. He must have been quite satisfied because he was not even looking the way we were moving so I concentrated on watching the taxiing path and other aircraft and carefully proceeded towards the starter's caravan. We stopped a hundred or so yards before the starting point to wait for someone to land and clear the runway. Whilst waiting, my instructor commented on my first flight at night, which apparently was not one of his most terrifying experiences. Next I had to do the cockpit drill and wait for the signal to go. We moved to the starting line and the whole performance was repeated. In all we did this seven times that night. I was gaining confidence and beginning to enjoy these excursions between the stars in the sky and the "stars" of the airfield when F.O. Krasnik decided that we had done enough. So, back to the hangar, then off to bed.

A few days later we had a few more circuits at night and then I was told to go on MY OWN! WOW!! Now I'll have to see and foresee everything all by myself! There will be nobody beside me to give the controls a nudge or ask me to correct the speed or direction or anything else. With my heart thumping louder than the engines I approached the starter's caravan and did the cockpit drill more like a prayer.

Green light! I rolled on to the runway, turned left and stopped. Green light flashed! Gradually opened throttles to full gas, kept to the middle of the flare path rolling faster and faster - tail is up - speed increases. Now my Oxford is attempting to leave the runway. Hold her down a bit longer until the speed is just above the recommended take off speed. Now gently lift her up and watch the instruments. All airfield lights disappeared behind me - keep the rate of climb steady and watch the compass. Reached 900ft then 1000ft, reduced gas to maintain the height. turned left and after a couple of minutes, left again. The sight of the flare path on my left was very reassuring. Moved downwind to the other end of the aerodrome to turn left again and again and so to start the final approach. Full concentration: watch the traffic lights, speed and direction - taking advantage of the most helpful flare path. Gently, gently - down until the wheels touch the runway and bounce and touch again, reduce gas and settle down to rolling slower and slower to turn and leave the runway.

Hurrah!! I've done it!! I'd like to shout but I find myself shaking with the sudden relaxation of all my nerves. Taxiing round the periphery to our dispersal point I found my instructor waiting for me. He signalled for me to stop then scrambled onto the wing and tapped on the window. I opened it to see his smiling face.

"Jak poszło?" – "How did it go?" he shouted over the steady rumble of the engines.

"Oh, all right" I answered trying to sound as if I had countless such escapades behind me. Just as well that we had to shout to each other for this covered the full excitement in my voice.

"Now do six more circuits and watch out. There are two other soloists like you in the air, I'll be waiting for you here". Then he scrambled down, walked to the front and waved me on. And so I became a night flyer!

It was well after midnight when I finally got into my bed, but I could not get to sleep. My mind was taking me back through the stages of learning to fly. Then further back through the training in the Warsaw Air Force College to be an Air Force Engineer. Yes! - Engineer! So what made me so determined to learn to fly? For the answer to that my memory flashed back to my school days when I was fourteen or fifteen.

We had our mid-term break and I was with my scout troop out in the fields marching back from an exercise when we saw an aircraft flying very low and next disappearing behind some bushes. We knew that there were no airfields in the vicinity. With utmost difficulty we complied with the Leader's order to march on. As soon as we reached our destination and got dismissed a few of us turned round and ran back to see the flying machine. We knew that such things existed, they could be seen near some major cities but to have one landing near our insignificant place was simply unbelievable! A unique chance to inspect it from close quarters.

That's what we hoped for, but by the time our little group reached the field the aircraft was not accessible. An army lorry was already there and a cordon of soldiers would not let any of us nearer than about 100 metres. So my dream of having a walk around and a close look at it, especially the propeller, and maybe touch it, had to remain a dream for about five years when I joined the Air Force and trained to qualify as engineer. Not as a pilot, because there was something not quite right with my eyesight. This looked like the final, irrevocable decision against my ambition to be able to fly. Lo and behold! Here I am on the point of qualifying as a pilot and what's more, good enough for <u>night flying</u>!

The next part of our training programme included formation flying. As usual - at first I had to do it with an instructor who showed me how to maintain the "stations" and how to follow the leader's manoeuvres. The day came when I was sent to do it on my own. This would have been nothing special except for the unusual behaviour of my Oxford. After take-off I tried to keep to my assigned position, slightly behind and to the left of the leader, but I had a heck of a job staying there. First one wing then the other dropped a little resulting in a gentle change of course. In spite of full correction on the controls it took a long time to recover. Puzzled and worried by the sluggish response I twisted the aileron's controls quite firmly one way and then the other only to find to my horror, that the wings did not respond in the slightest and that the controls felt unusually free. "Hey!! What's happened?" I tried again - no response. Next I tested the pedals: left - the aircraft drifted to the left trying to make a rather clumsy turn. I realised that I could not possibly carry on with the formation flying exercise. My hands were too busy trying to correct the deviations by using the engines to hold the course - I could not radio the leader to tell him that I had to attempt an immediate return to base. For a fleeting moment a panicky thought tried to take control of my mind.

"Jump...abandon the kite!! You'll never make it!!" – Ideas like that flashed through my mind. Although my Oxford was misbehaving it was not going into a spin and was flying quite steadily. What's more the weather was being very kind to me, no bumps and only a gentle breeze. I started visualising the triumph if I somehow managed to bring the aircraft down safely.

So my first task was to find out to what degree the controls were useless. With great relief I found that the tail was responding to the rudder so it was only the ailerons that did not work. All right - let us try turning using the engines and the rudder. So, left pedal forward and reduce gas on the port engine. This made the port wing dip and the turn was not too dreadful. Next, try it the other way...not so bad. I tried these tests again and each change of direction gave me more confidence. Now let's get back to the aerodrome. When I was within sight of the control tower I radioed in that I had to carry out an emergency landing.

"Partial failure of controls" I reported.

"Come in" was the reply, "the field is clear for you". All other planes were ordered to keep away as I gingerly began to turn and prayed that no sudden gust of wind would jerk one wing up. I could see the fire engine racing to the mid-field position followed by an ambulance.

"No panic!" I thought to myself. "The situation is not so critical. Just let me get on with it." By now I had enough confidence in controlling my naughty Oxford to continue the approach without watching the instruments too closely. It was much more important not to allow any drifting out of line with the runway, especially towards the hangars and to some aircraft parked near them. I knew that I had to land at the first attempt - there was no chance of a second go. Playing with the engines and the rudder and with a lot of sweating and swearing I finally touched the ground. What a relief! Taxiing towards our squadrons' hangar I could see just about the whole ground crew awaiting me but when the C.O. appeared the crowd scattered to their jobs. Finally guided by signals from a mechanic I parked the plane in the right place. I got down and reported in detail to the C.O. what had happened. In the meantime the mechanics uncovered the area under the cockpit where the control wires and pulleys were visible. The sprocket was dangling free - completely disconnected from the rest of the installation. I wanted to get nearer and see the damage more closely but the C.O. called me away and ordered me to take another Oxford and take off to join the other planes with which I was practising formation flying. They were circling above obviously waiting for me. I think that my C.O. was a bit of a psychologist. He knew that some trainees could lose their nerve so this could be normal practice and the best medicine - not to give the pilot time or chance to think about the incident. Well, so much for the "hero's welcome" but this did not prevent me giving a very graphic account to my pals (with some embellishments!) when we gathered in the mess for a drink.

Our life during flying training was not restricted to the airfield, the classroom, the officers' mess or our quarters. We had our days out and the city of Nottingham had its attractions in spite of wartime restrictions. There were cinemas, bars, and dance halls but more importantly there were also quite friendly girls. On one of our visits to such a dance hall Romek and I met Audrey and Pat. A few dances and a few drinks and we were quite good friends. A few weeks later and after a few visits to cinemas we were on kissing terms. Our aspirations received a boost when we discovered that they were only billeted in Nottingham, their homes were further South in Bedford or Luton. Romek and I started planning a "holiday weekend" in a hotel in Nottingham or some other town, but this idea was not enthusiastically received by the girls. Obviously we had to use longer-term tactics - more dances and visits to the bars. The softening up process was proceeding quite well when I was told that I had completed the course and in two days time I was to report for a pre-operational course at a training centre for navigators. This, I was told, was an essential part of the training for pilots going on long-range missions. Fair enough...just so long as I was not expected to become a navigator myself.

My next meeting with Pat was a very sad one. We were on the platform when my train arrived and I told her that this was the beginning of the "hot" war for me and that there would be little chance for us to meet any more. To my horror she broke into tears! I had no idea that this sweet girl was taking our friendship so seriously. I tried to explain that too many chaps did not come back from raids on Germany and that it would not be fair to have her worrying for...months...not knowing...when...?!! She seemed to accept the reasoning but only partially.

"Will you write to me, say, once a month, just to say you are alright. Not much to ask, is it?" she implored.

A very difficult situation. By now I was quite fond of her, but... every now and then during the last two years we had heard very sad accounts from our instructors who finished their "ops" tours and were having a rest by training us. These sad cases were increasing as the bombing raids intensified. My mind was made up. I just could not have any emotional ties while I was on operational training or duties.

"Sorry, my dear Pat but I must have my mind and my heart free, so I cannot promise to keep in touch".

I felt a heel saying that but I just had to make a complete break there and then. The train was about to start so one more rather tearful kiss and I hopped in, shut the door and leaned out to wave goodbye. The poor girl was trying to use her handkerchief for both waving and drying her tears. My heart felt sore and I had to fight the temptation to jump out to take her in my arms and promise more than just letters.

Imagine my disgust when I found that it was not me who would be trained. At this airfield in Wales other chaps were trained to become navigators while all I was expected to do was to be kind of a "coach driver" who takes groups of trainees for trips over the countryside. My bitter complaints to the C.O. were mellowed when he patiently explained:

"Primo - to be a proficient, operational, long range pilot you have to put in many more hours of flying in all sorts of weather; and Secundo - someone has to help me train navigators. One of them may one day be responsible for finding a safe route for your aircraft to get you back home. He has got to have lots of air experience and for that we need pilots to carry them all over the country". After a couple of weeks I felt quite chuffed to be sitting at the table marked "Staff"!

My service there lasted from mid-November 1942 to September '43. The planes we used were Avro Ansons, twin-engined machines capable of carrying four pupils. My job as a Staff Pilot was to take a crew of 2 or 3 for a flight to an assigned target. The crew would be trainee navigators who had to apply their theoretical training in the classroom to a practical flight to the target. Their job would be to give me direction - a course to steer to find the target and "bomb it". In practice the bombing of a target meant taking a photograph of a bridge or a railway yard or station, or crossroads, etc. The main factors to be taken into consideration would be the speed of the aircraft as well as the wind speed and direction and the distance to the target. The course to steer was important but equally important was the E.T.A. (estimated time of arrival). In poor visibility the E.T.A. was essential. Such flights lasted from about an hour with beginners to well over two hours with more advanced trainee navigators. Quite often I had two such trips in one day.

Living conditions were quite good but outside the camp there was very little unless one took the bus to Criccieth. I soon chummed up with another pilot named Witek [pronounced Veetek] and together we made excursions into the town. He had already discovered a hotel where he felt more or less at home and on some weekends he did not bother returning to the camp. When I saw his vivacious, dark eyed, black-haired girl I felt quite envious and tried to find a welcoming pair of arms for myself. There were some girls who felt "abandoned" whilst their husbands were "somewhere" serving their country and I nearly made a fool of myself with one of them but by sheer luck or by a twist of events I did not get involved to any extent...but my appetite was whetted.

Whilst on the airfield my eyes were also "set a-roving". This must have been noticed by a very attractive WAAF who gave me an encouraging smile when I had to visit the office in which she worked. I soon found an excuse for another visit, and then another. Then I discovered that occasionally she had to return after official hours to catch up with her work. By then it was midwinter, so blinds had to be drawn and all we had to do was to lock the door and we had a snug place for most un-office-like activities. Jane (let that be her name) was unattached and found the camp life as incomplete as I did, so her 'overtime work' became more and more frequent. In the spring we managed to organise a couple of bicycles, which enabled us to make excursions to Abersoch, Aberdaren and other villages.

One day we stayed too long and had to cycle back after dark. I tried to get some glimmer of light out of my lamp - but in vain. Jane's lamp produced the regulation glow so I did not worry and we proceeded happily, only to be stopped by a man. He had a band on his arm pronouncing him to be Homeguard or Special Constable or something of the sort. He was most indignant that I had no light and I could not convince him that in the blackout situation surely the less light the better. He was determined to make an issue of it and wanted to report me to the local police and also to the Camp Commander. Suddenly Jane broke into beautiful Welsh and from that moment I could only look in amazement as they were 'singing' in Welsh to each other. The result was that the 'officious official' finally shrugged his shoulders and left us. I asked Jane what it was all about. She just laughed.

Days later, while chatting about things with another pilot who was English, I mentioned this incident and his comment was most unexpected. Apparently some Welsh people were not too happy having RAF or any other military establishments on Welsh soil. This seemed incredible to me...I just could not believe that there were people in this country who would disagree with the paramount necessity to fight Nazism, or at least to defend the last outpost in Europe resisting the foul flood.

The weather was exceptional so I was sent for the third time in one day with a crew of three pupils on a navigation exercise. The first navigator managed to guide me to our objective very well...a rather small railway bridge on Anglesey Island. The second pupil had some difficulty in getting us to the second target that was a road junction near Denbigh. With a little discussion and correction we finally got there and secured the evidence ie: our second photograph. The last objective was even more difficult since it was set for the most advanced pupil of my crew. This was to be a low level bombing run from a village called Maesbrook, due South of Oswestry. The navigator, using large-scale maps, had to prepare his route and to pre-calculate our E.T.A. to make sure that we attacked our target on the first attempt. We came down from 5000 to about 200ft and followed a road leading west to Lake Vyrnwy. The object of the exercise was to take a photograph of a hotel at the head of the lake. In the bombing run the pupil had to be in the bomb-aimer's position, i.e. in the nose of the aircraft. Map in hand, he had to give me course corrections.

The sudden change of height produced a dramatic change to the landscape ahead. Whilst flying high one can see an area of a few miles radius quite clearly with many more miles of less clear background but map reading goes to pot when skimming over the fields at almost tree level! Landmarks appear and disappear before one can make any reference to the map. A thin line of trees ahead looks like the edge of a forest. Lakes and villages have distorted dimensions, so no wonder that we were on the wrong track within minutes. A little later, when the exact minute of our E.T.A. passed, the hapless pupil admitted that he must have missed an important landmark. The mountains were approaching rapidly so full throttle, back to 5000 ft and I took him back to the starting point of the low-level run and we tried again. This time he made a perfect job of it. We followed the correct fork of the road and almost immediately the glistening surface of the lake appeared between the hills. He knew that our target, the hotel, was behind the hill on the right bank of the lake. In my earphones I could hear calm instructions:

"Right...right...steady" followed by a rapid "Left...left...steady ...steady...BOMBS GONE!!" - meaning photograph taken. Beaming with proud satisfaction he crawled out and settled down with the others to work out the course home.

Low level flying is very exciting so I took them the full length of the lake as low as possible by way of reward. The fun lasted only a couple of minutes before we had to climb back to 5000ft and set our course for base. Below us was a thin layer of cloud and at least 1000ft above us was another much heavier layer. Here and there columns of clouds, like pillars, were rising from the lower layer right up to the top layer. The sun was very low, thus illuminating the higher cloud from underneath and the effect was astounding. We were in a colossal cathedral! Columns on both sides with colours from white to light grey whilst the ceiling was blazing gold with touches of pink and red. By then we were above the bay so the 'floor cloud' had a light green tint. Everyone was quiet as if praying and I wished we could have stayed there for a while, suspended in this enchanting world.

I was becoming very familiar and even attached to the great

variety of landmarks and to the beauty of this countryside but that pleasure did not diminish the feeling of being left on a side track. One after another, groups of my pupils were leaving the Station and even my one and only compatriot had left a couple of months ago. By now most of them were probably in serious action speeding up the end of this war and bringing nearer the day when all Polish squadrons would be free to fly back to their airfields at home. And all that was happening without my front line contribution! What a sight it would be for my poor, tormented, devastated fatherland; for my parents and family and our friends - to see squadron after squadron coming back home with the Polish red and white checkerboards painted on the aircraft. What a welcome!

"Now, now, don't get too emotional". There was still an immense job to be done there and then. To cheer me up I could see the total number of my flying hours growing rapidly. By mid-September I had over 600 hours in the air, of which at least 400 were as a staff pilot with valuable experience for future operational work.

On the right path...At last!

The authorities must have been waiting for that magic number of "400", because within days I was posted to a training station near Blackpool to take a course in reconnaissance and <u>navigation</u>!! The only difference being that part of it was with night flying which added astro-navigation to my experience. Fortunately it did not take very long. The course completed and then another posting...I found myself in an operational squadron towards the end of 1943.

This was the 304 Squadron in Cornwall, originally one of the Polish squadrons in Bomber Command and its aircraft was the Vickers Wellington. In May 1943 it changed base from Lindholme to Tiree in the Inner Hebrides and only a month later it was moved to Dale in South Wales. As if those two rapid changes of base were not enough, it found itself established in Predannack in South West Cornwall by the end of the year, one of the best stations for keeping an eye on the South Western Approaches.

So at last I was a pilot in a squadron that was for fighting the enemy and not just training crews. America was now getting seriously involved by sending a colossal tonnage of war equipment and thousands of troops by sea. The Atlantic became a good hunting ground for the U-boats operating against Allied shipping as well as for the Royal Navy and Coastal Command against those German submarines. The action started hotting up. Whilst only in my first month and as the second pilot I had the privilege to sweep Western Approaches searching for any signs of U-boats. My duty was to share the hours of flying the Wellington with the First Pilot. The duration of our flights was between 9 and 10 hours and almost exclusively at night. Night patrolling was our speciality, for which the Wellington was initially equipped with a powerful searchlight and later with radar.

At the beginning of January I had my first thrilling experience of attacking a U-boat after about four, rather boring hours flying on our usual route towards Spain at some distance from the French coast. Our radar operator reported: "contact - 30 miles", which meant there was something worth investigating. Next he gave a correction for the course by a few degrees west. You could feel the atmosphere within the fuselage changing from a rather relaxed, bored but watchful one, to all eyes and ears on full alert! The radar was still showing the 'contact' with a steadily reducing distance. Next the Captain asked the bomb aimer (bombs = depth charges) to get into his position. The rear gunner had to be more watchful than ever because the radar operator was now almost exclusively interested in the 'contact'. Everybody was ready and hoped that the 'contact' would be a U-boat.

The situation was very much like the "cat and mouse" scenario. We - the cat - were trying to get swiftly into position with our 'teeth and claws' ie: depth charges and machine guns ready to pounce on the 'mouse' whilst it was looking for the 'piece of cheese' ie: the helpless merchant vessel carrying something useful for our war effort. The 'contact' was still on the screen so the Captain opened the bomb doors. The tension was almost unbearable. Our position together with our readiness to attack was reported to the base. By now the 'contact object' was only about two miles ahead. Our searchlight was switched on and the beam swept the sea in front of us. The bomb aimer called:

"U-boat !!....right...right...steady...BOMBS GONE!!"

The U-boat, of course, had someone on guard on the conning tower looking out and listening for aircraft like ours. We must have been spotted as the searchlight was switched on, so within seconds the U-boat went into a "crash-dive." The effect was that our depth charges were falling on an almost fully submerged submarine.

Next, the area had to be marked with a flare, so that we could turn back and search the right area for possible evidence of success as thoroughly as possible. Also, there was always a chance that a Royal Navy ship might not be far away and could be alerted by our base. We made a number of sweeps without spotting anything of importance. The Captain had to watch the time and the fuel reserves. Also, we were almost useless without any more depth charges, so after about half an hour waiting for any directive from base we set a course for home.

One could easily form the opinion that I had no useful function at all in this performance. Actually I did feel like a spare part (with a label 'just-in-case') in an efficient machine. My insignificant (at first glance) duty was to watch the radio altimeter since the First Pilot's eyes were straining to see the U-boat which we were attacking at only about 100ft above sea level. Also I had to wait for the order to drop the flare through its chute.

At the beginning of March our squadron had to transfer to Chivenor in north Devon. Not far away. A few weeks later there was some talk that the U-boats were getting daringly impudent and trying to penetrate into St George's Channel. The weather was dreadful...low cloud with some snow and even suspicions of frost in the air. Normally this would be "no flying weather", but such menacing audacity by the Germans required immediate action. Our position in Devon, was the best for keeping an eye on the channel between Devon and Cork in Ireland. Of course it was just our 'luck' to be on stand-by that day so we were given this task. We took off early in the evening with a strong north-westerly wind making our take-off awkward. Almost as soon as we left the runway we were in the cloud. Visibility nil! - completely!! From now we had to rely entirely on our radar and the compass. With the aircraft thrown about by the wind the compass was never steady and to make matters worse the radar operator was not too happy with his machine.

I was at the controls on our first Devon - Cork return-trip. In the atrocious weather our aircraft was hardly ever flying on steady course or at the same height. This kind of flying is very tiring so we, the pilots, decided to shorten our turns at the controls to one and one-half hours. After about 8 hours of this tedious and futile looking out for the submarine the Captain decided to obtain 'the fix' of our position. He went to consult with the radar operator - I was at the controls – and I heard him shout out "Impossible! Check again". Our position was confirmed. Imagine our amazement and horror when we found ourselves somewhere west of Brest!! That meant that the northerly wind had become a gale.

It also meant that we would need at least 3 hours to get back to the base since our 'land speed' would have to take into account the most economical fuel consumption and the effect of the wind blowing against us. So first - the load had to be reduced by jettisoning the depth charges. Next - the shortest course to be taken without coming too near to Brest. The petrol gauges were not promising us three hours in the air so the dreaded routine of emergency landing (on water!) had to be refreshed in our minds, e.g. inflating our safety belts, loosening ties, releasing and inflating the dinghy without letting it float away, checking that all emergency equipment was to hand, reporting our ditching position etc. After another hour our position was reported and we received orders to take course for Predannack, which would save us about 100 miles. One could just about feel everybody's mind willing the miles away and praying that we reached the beaches or at least some suitable field. Ten hours passed - the petrol gauges were looking grim! Eleventh hour in the air - port engine started 'coughing'! Petrol in the main tanks all gone! Switch over to small emergency tanks which, with luck, would give us about half an hour extra - no more! Radar showing land 30 miles slightly east of north. Minutes passing but nothing visible. Suddenly the First Pilot, who was standing with his head in the astro-dome, shouted out "light ahead". This must be Predannack expecting us and trying to help. A little nearer and the 'traffic lights" at the end of the runway were visible. Only a couple of miles more! "Oh God - please help us". Engines still behaving. Time to reduce height and speed...a little lower and TOUCHING THE EARTH!!! WE HAVE BEEN SAVED!! THANK YOU ALMIGHTY!! Our Wellington is rolling. Loss of speed allows the tail to touch the ground. "What's happening!?" Engines coughing again and within seconds both engines stop!

Apparently the fact that the aircraft's position changed from horizontal, (flying or fast rolling), to 'three points' on the runway or 'nose up' angle, the petrol, or what was left of it, could not use gravity to flow any more. Our tow-tractor arrived quickly to clear us of the runway and to take us to the refuelling point. At the same time our generous 'emergency hosts' invited us to a good breakfast. This did not take very long, so we took off for our base with the daybreak wondering what kind of reception was awaiting us in the debriefing session. We were very tired when we landed at home. After all - it was 14 hours ago when we left this place. The debriefing officers must have seen our exhaustion so after brief questioning, sent us to bed advising us to stay there for at least eight hours.

The next few days were spent on improving our skills in homing, in radar navigation, in bombing, etc. and again we were ready to resume our routine A/S (anti-submarine) sweeps. The weather was not in a hurry to improve and my operational flying hours were only creeping up very slowly as a result. I required at least 80 additional hours to be promoted to the position of the First Pilot and take charge of the aircraft.

On the 26th of March it was our turn to take off for an A/S sweep. About three hours after the take off the First Pilot (or Captain) asked me to take over the controls from him for the next two hours. This was the routine on most of our flights, especially on the operational ones. We continued in silence, everyone concentrating in readiness for instant action. We were peacefully proceeding towards Spain when less than half an hour later the radar operator reported two contacts behind us.

" Contact! Directly behind us. About 20 miles."

The semi-relaxed atmosphere sharpened up immediately. The Captain called out:

"Rear gunner - report immediately you see anything!"

"Navigator - take exact reading of our position!"

"Radio - stand by!"

My muscles tensed up waiting for the report from the radar about the distance between them and us. In a couple of minutes he told us that the distance had decreased! This information was alarming - it proved that they were not a couple of fishing boats. Since the distance was slowly and inexorably decreasing - they must be aircraft! In our briefing there was no mention of any of our aircraft operating in this area so they must be German!! Let's speed up then and turn west, away from France. They will be night-fighters so they will not be too keen to fly away from land since they must have spent some time and fuel searching the area. Now the rear gunner reported:

"I can see two faintly glowing lights. One is directly behind: 6 o'clock and the other is at 7 o'clock and higher".

(This "6 o'clock" method is used to indicate direction in relation to our aircraft which is visualised as placed in the centre of the clock and flying towards the 12 o'clock hour.)

"Have you got one of them in your gun-sights? Take aim and be ready to fire when I count to three. I'll be turning right. READY?"

"Yes Sir" he answered.

"Right - one, two, THREE!! I shouted and pushed my right foot forward and started tilting the right wing down. At the same time I heard the rattle of our machine guns and almost simultaneously I saw a large number of small points of flame all round us - flying faster than our Wellington!!

"Heavens above!" I cried seeing some of them penetrating the left wing which was tilted upwards and clearly visible.

"Oh Lord - not the incendiaries - PLEASE!" remembering the petrol tanks installed in both wings.

Our Captain was at the same time giving orders to the radio operator to contact our headquarters to give them our position and to report the attack by the German night fighters. We were still turning to our desired course, West, when a sudden strong flash illuminated our aircraft. I could see that we were not the source of the flash when the rear gunner, almost together with the Captain, shouted out:

"ONE SHOT DOWN !!"

After that I thought I could hear the gunner swearing and muttering something to himself but all I wanted to know was:

" Where is the other German?"

I did not get the answer from the gunner but from the Captain:

"He disappeared as fast as he could...thanks to our brave rear-gunner"

I was sure that the German would have reported their fruitless attack to his command by now and also giving them our position and direction of flight hoping that an interception could be organised. We were now moving fast in the northerly direction to get round the Brest Peninsula. Our navigator informed us that in about 45 minutes we should be flying past it which would make us feel safer. Surely - there might be our night fighters meeting us. The radar operator had to make sure that nothing was following us but even more carefully spot anything coming from the French coast on our right.

The Captain came to tell me that our brave gunner had his left ear badly damaged in the exchange of gun fire and that as he was looking after the poor chap I would have to remain at the controls quite a bit longer. Only one inch away from losing his life! That thought made me shudder!

Being decorated with the 'Virtuti militari' cross

Thinking about our wounded member of the crew a thought flashed in my mind of the days in West Frough, Scotland, when I was involved in training the air gunners. Was he there at the same time, learning air gunnery? That would make my very unwanted posting much more acceptable. It would not be such a useless delay in my progress to the part I wanted to play in this war.

At this point the radar operator reported that we were 55 miles west of a small island which is only 12 miles off the French coast near Brest. So this meant one more hour of flying but with fast improving safety. The tense atmosphere in the aircraft gradually relaxing to the extent of us having badly wanted sandwiches.

We landed about an hour after midnight and were greeted like heroes by the night shift staff. The ambulance took the wounded gunner to the sick bay, while the rest of us spent half an hour on debriefing and another half an hour on our badly wanted breakfast. Then...TO BED! It took me a while to get my mind off our "meeting" with the German night fighters and get to sleep.

After a day of complete rest I had to take the first part of the test which would qualify me to become the First Pilot. The test proved that I had had enough practice in controlling the aircraft so during the next few days I had to take off with a crew of two or three to carry out a variety of tasks like circuits and landings, "bombing", radar exercises etc. Finally I had to take off "solo" - on my own - and perform circuits and landings for about an hour and half.

Even all that was not enough to obtain the title: "First Pilot" for operational purposes. So, during the next seven weeks I had to gain more experience in the same kind of flights but this time with full crews, taking command as the First Pilot. Finally, one fully operational A/S sweep of 10 hours - five in daylight and five after sunset - under my command made me the First Pilot. That was on 26th June 1944.

In my Flying Officer Uniform

During the next six months, four at Chivenor and two on Benbecula Island (we transferred to Benbecula, a Scottish island in the Outer Hebrides on the 21st September), I built up my total number of operational flying to 453 hours in 48 sorties.

This statement appears in my logbook:

COMPLETED FIRST OPERATIONAL TOUR IN COASTAL COMMAND
From Dec. 19th 1943 to Dec. 12th 1944

sorties 48, hours 453,10 min.

Why Benbecula you might ask? Was our squadron trying to get far away from the D-Day work and danger? No, not at all!

In 1943 the German progress in Russia suffered a severe setback at Stalingrad. This was followed by general slowing down which gradually changed into retreat. Hitler and his "Intelligence Office" must have never heard of Napoleon's well known experience. He completely neglected to take heed of the annual demonstration of the determined defence of Russia by her faithful ally called "General Frost". This was followed by the further and fatal weakness in Hitler's intelligence, namely in failing to discover the imminent danger of Great Britain's and her Allies' readiness to invade Europe!

The effect of the preparations and of the actual D-Day on our squadron was that we had to leave Predannack for the use of squadrons directly involved in the D-Day action. On 1st March '44 we had to jump from Predannack to Chivenor and, for similar reasons, seven months later from Chivenor to Benbecula. After D-Day in June '44 the German Navy had just about no chance to operate from the French ports, whether with ships or with submarines. They tried to continue their naval activities from their Baltic ports by sneaking out between Denmark and Norway to attack the convoys carrying supplies to Russia. Therefore some of the Coastal Command squadrons had to be moved north and 304 Squadron landed on Benbecula.

The airfield was placed on the western edge of the island, not that there was much choice with the size of the place. One of the first things that we had to learn was to practice a special style of walking. You just couldn't take the normal, natural, upright posture. The very strong wind, mainly from the West, meant that you had to walk with your body leaning against it and your face turned to avoid the violent gusts but your eyes set on the direction you wanted to proceed. The only positive and quite important advantage this kind of wind gave us was that, since most of our takeoffs were westwards, they were shorter. To have to use the runway right to the edge of the island was really nerve-wracking!

The Officers Mess and our bedroom huts were quite satisfactory. Our separation from the rest of the world occasionally created quite a strong yearning for a town, or even village life with shops, buses, pubs, churches and with people in "civvies" moving about. Not just the same faces in the same uniforms every day.

My eleven patrols from this island did not add anything operationally exciting but some of the night patrols gave us the rare chance to admire the Aurora Borealis in her full glory (a luminous electric phenomenon radiating from the earth's magnetic northern pole - I am explaining this to save you searching for your Oxford Dictionary). This pleasure required very strong self-discipline to avoid becoming mesmerised by this magnetic display between the sky and the sea and to neglect our primary duty of watching out for the damned U-boats.

Completion of my First Operational Tour was followed by transfer to a new base to have a rest on a good spell of leave. Thus, about mid-December I left Benbecula and travelled all the way to Silloth R.A.F. base west of Carlisle. This was near to such places as the Lake District, Lancaster and Blackpool. So before Christmas I went to

Blackpool to refresh my acquaintance with the town and some friendly faces. I had an invitation to Lancaster from my best friends, Norah and Alan for Christmas where I had a jolly good time and a good rest.

Upon returning to Silloth, I found myself busy doing "circuits and landings" with new pilots requiring practice and other flights like aircraft test, weather test and so on. The war was quite obviously running to its end and on 28th March 1945 I had my last flight and was given a few days leave.

Standing outside our squadron office with my boss, F. L. Piotrowski – Silloth 1944/5

Spring 1945

When I contacted Norah by telephone she said, without any hesitation, that my room would be ready on Tuesday and informed me that Alan's birthday was on 4th April. My journey from Silloth was quick and easy. Very conveniently, the bus from Lancaster, took me all the way from the station almost to the door of their home, Cartref. There as usual, a warm welcome was waiting for me, with a cup of tea and a promise of a meal as soon as Alan came home. A couple of hours later Alan arrived and when we sat down he mentioned his birthday on Thursday and invited me to join him on a business trip to Coniston. He had to deliver a pair of new boots to a nearby farmer.

"On the way back we'll stop at Sunny Bank for a night or two. I'll take a day off since it is my birthday."

"That will be lovely!" I exclaimed. I was very pleased with the chance to admire more of the lovely Lakeland.

On Thursday it took Alan a couple of hours to read his extra large mail and discuss it with Norah and then we set off at about 10 o'clock. Every few miles Alan gave me a brief commentary on the area and at Coniston we stopped for a cup of coffee. Not many miles further on we found the farm we were looking for and delivered a pair of boots. The farmer was so pleased with his boots that he tried to persuade Alan to accept his wife's invitation for lunch.

"I am very sorry" said Alan "But I have to be at Sunny Bank for lunch, that's just under a mile past Torver, and later on for my Birthday Party!" So, after a lot of laughter and birthday wishes we left and about half an hour later we reached the guesthouse where we were greeted by the owners, Bessie and Ted. Whilst introducing me to them, Alan added:

"Ted is Jack's brother and Jack's cousin, Dorothy, is staying here on her convalescence leave."

After that we were shown to our rooms and a while later I set off to go down to the lounge from where I could hear the voices of a group of people discussing something noisily but cheerfully. On the last two steps I suddenly stopped! What stopped me was a vision of a very pretty girl sitting under the window with a view of a grassy bank, trees and a stream as a background. She was quite still and seemed to be looking at her book rather than reading it. She must have heard me coming down as she lifted her eyes toward me when I stopped.

Now! - If you do not believe in the stories about the angel called Cupid and his arrows then I can tell you that his arrows were flying with fantastic effect! When our eyes met I suddenly felt a powerful pull towards the point from which the arrow flew - the girl's eyes!! What cruelly brought me down to earth was Alan's voice right near to my face urging me to come with him to meet his friends - the noisy group. After those introductions he brought me back and said,

"And this is Dorothy Postlethwaite, Jack's cousin "

After that he left us - to my huge satisfaction! My heart was still vibrating so I heard the name Dorothy but after that just something like the sounds of letters; "p, tl, thw" but actually I just could not concentrate on exchanging names. I said something to Dorothy, commenting on the beauty of the scene behind her - just to start a conversation, to which she responded with a lovely shy smile. I confidently took this as a permission to sit down near her. A chair was standing nearby so I brought it nearer and sat down. She looked at the label with Poland on my sleeve and asked:

"When did you come to England?"

"About five years ago." I answered briefly.

I did not want to start on this subject knowing that it would take far too long. So I said "Have you been actively engaged in the war effort?"

"My profession is nursing and as you must have heard I am here on convalescence leave." she answered.

"Oh! Why? What happened?"

"Nothing very serious. Mainly due to the great load of work and poor conditions"

I had a feeling that there must be more to it. Was she injured? But I could see that she would rather leave this subject. So we just chatted, mainly about the lakes, like Coniston and Windermere and the hills not far away, like The Old Man of Coniston (rather funny name I thought) and Weatherlam. It was quite obvious to me that she was longing to visit them again but not in her present condition.

The next day Alan and his party decided to take a walk after the lunch along the lake to some café for ice creams. Since Dorothy was obviously not fit enough for such exercise I suggested taking her there in a rowing boat. First I had to find Ted and ask him whether I could borrow his boat and whether my idea was sensible considering Dorothy's health.

"Oh yes! She'll enjoy it. The boat is moored at the mouth of the brook and the oars are in the garage. Help yourself." was Ted's answer.

"Thank you very much. Are there any restrictions visible or not visible on our route to the "ice cream village?" I had to make sure.

"Nothing unusual on route but it is a long way to Nibthwaite so you'll be very tired by the time you get back." Ted warned me. I found Dorothy in the kitchen talking to Bessie. They both turned to me to hear my report about the proposed "boat trip".

"The weather is just right;" Bessie commented. "not raining and not expected to rain according to the forecast for today."

"So, Dorothy, do you feel like going?" I asked.

"Oh yes! I'll just put something warmer on and take my rollup mac, without which I do not venture out in the Lakes. I'll be back in a minute".

"I'll get a couple of sandwiches ready." Bessie said to me. "And a flask of tea. I heard Ted say that it may take you well over an hour to get anywhere near Nibthwaite and the same to get back here for the evening meal."

"That is a very good and very generous idea. Thank you very much." I said and dashed off to the garage to find the oars. When I got back to our meeting point Dorothy was already there.

"See you later!" she called out to Ted and Bessie.

"Have good time!" they answered as we set off.

The path has obviously been well used and our progress for about ten minutes was quite good. When we reached some trees and shrubs Dorothy said:

"We turn left here. This path leads to another house further down".

The footpath changed completely. High and wet grass together with the shrubs made our progress quite slow. When we reached the lake I said to Dorothy:

"Please, stop for a minute. I'll put these things in the boat and drag it into an easier position for embarkation." I untied the rope and pushed and pulled until the boat was more accessible and easier to turn it around and sail away. Next I offered my hand to help her get in and to sit down. As she touched my hand I felt a warm wave going through my body.

"Is this Cupid playing his tricks again?" I asked myself. I pushed the boat off the sand and scrambled in. At last we were on the way so I said to my passenger:

"Please look out for any boat or anything that might be in our way."

After only a few strokes with the oars the whole expanse of the lake became visible. Right across, near the other side of the lake, I could see a small island.

"An island over there!" I called out pointing across the lake.

"Yes, this is Peel Island" she told me.

"Could we have a look?" I asked hoping that she would not be very disappointed if we did not get as far as Nibthwaite and miss the ice creams as a result. After all - it would take at least an hour of hard rowing to get there and another hour to get back. In the ice cream place we would be in a noisy group not giving us a chance to have a quiet "tete a tete".

Dorothy just shrugged her shoulders with a little grin and said nothing, which I interpreted as "Its up to you", so of course, I steered to Peel Island without delay. It took me about quarter of an hour to get near it. I had to twist round to look for a place suitable for landing. All I could see was rocks with trees above them. Rowing slowly round I was looking for at least a small gap between not too high rocks to be able to scramble up. After all Dorothy's fitness had to be considered.

"Oh! Here is something we could try." I called out seeing a patch of gravel with lower rocks than the rest. When we crunched to a stop I jumped out to pull the boat in as much as possible and make it really steady. Dorothy got up and came forward to grasp my hand for disembarking. She managed that quite well. I jerked the boat a few more inches forward, grabbed the rope and threw it towards the nearest tree above us. Next I helped my companion to get on top of the lowest rock, got myself up and tied the rope to that tree.

The first yard or so of the surface of the island was quite rough with deep cracks in the rock so I kept close to Dorothy just in case. But she very bravely crossed over to a small clear space. We walked round it to get the view in all directions. The best view was in the northerly direction. With the sun behind us the lake and the hills were perfectly illuminated for photography but, unfortunately, we had no camera with us.

Dorothy started describing the view explaining which hill was 'The Old Man of Coniston' (I'd like to know the history of this name) and which was 'The Weatherlam' and how she loved walking in this area with so many pretty streams, bridges and waterfalls. Their family home being in Barrow-in-Furness they all had many happy days in the Lakes. She must have been to all corners of Lakeland with her parents and two brothers, all of whom were keen walkers.

Her enthusiastic description of the view revived my appetite for such walks which was re-ignited a year or two earlier by Nora and Alan with Jack and Vin who took me to see Windermere Lake and to the top of Helvelyn and so on. My expeditions to the Tatra Mountains in Poland were very impressive with their rocky heights but not as beautiful as the Lake District

I could see Dorothy looking right and left - obviously looking for somewhere to sit down. The time had reached about 3pm and all this talk about lakes, streams and waterfalls made us thirsty. The sandwiches and the tea were quite quickly consumed but somehow neither of us showed any signs of readiness to proceed towards the boat. We felt comfortably warm and for a few minutes we sat silent when Dorothy asked me to tell her something about Poland and how I got to England.

I asked her "Could you, in your mind, see the central part of Europe starting with Germany? The next country, moving East, we get into Poland and next into Russia. South of Poland was Czechoslovakia and on it's East end, Romania. My squadron was based next to the town Kraków (Cracoof phonetically) which is almost due south from Warsaw towards the Tatras and to Czechoslovakia. A very easy and tempting target for the Luftwaffe."

Here I glanced at my watch - it was nearly quarter past four. This meant that I had no more than half an hour to finish my story. Hoping that Dorothy would not have any difficulty in visualising that part of Europe I started "travelling" at a high speed to the south/east corner of Poland, hoping to make contact with what was left of my squadron which must have been persistently, frequently and ruthlessly attacked.

"The main task of my unit was to keep in touch with our squadron and to be available for repairs of any damage to the aircraft. The squadron, or what was "left of it" after the first, horrible, early morning air raid, left very quickly."

Next, full of horrible feelings, a few words about our surrender on the Romanian border followed by internment and the escape to France.

"We did not stay in France longer than eight months. In June Germans were marching into Paris and we had to "run" to Port Vendre on the coast of the Mediterranean Sea. From there we had to sail to Algeria, then by train to Casablanca and sail to Gibraltar. There we joined a long convoy which took nearly a fortnight to get us to Liverpool on July 12th 1940 (a very important date for me).

My next glance at my watch made me jump. It was a few minutes past five o'clock and we had to be back at Sunny Bank at about quarter to six for a quick wash and change and to get downstairs for our evening meal. I got off my rocky stool wondering whether she could do with a little bit of help. She started getting up rather slowly and with some hesitation so I went to her with both my hands on offer to help. She accepted them rather firmly and slid off the rock with a deep sigh. My hands wouldn't let her go but gently helped her to take the first step forward... towards me. I moved slightly forward, then...embraced her firmly and...KISSED HER ! She did not resist, her face was not saying "Please stop!" so, of course, I did not stop...I simply could not stop! The sweet girl did not show any signs of repulsion but with a twinkle in her eyes and a shy smile turned to leave the island. When we reached the point of descending onto the little beach and the boat I had to jump forward to get down first to help her to join me and into the boat. The crossing over and walking towards the Sunny Bank seemed to take less time than the same trip took earlier in the day. We arrived just as the walking party started assembling round the table.

"Hello you two! Did you get lost? We did not see you at Nibthwaite!" shouted Alan laughing.

"Oh - I spotted a lovely island just right for a rest and a picnic." I answered.

"Please give us a minute and we'll join you." added Dorothy.

As we were returning to the group at the table I could see their smiling faces turning from Dorothy to me and vice versa quite obviously trying to assess the progress in our friendship. This was followed by a bit of teasing. After all "a young couple on a lonely island...hmm...hmm" thoughts like that must have been spinning in their minds. When they discovered that most of the tine on the island was spent on a very much abbreviated description of my escape from Poland they started calling from all directions to give them a brief report. I just couldn't wriggle out of that so I said:

"To describe the route alone as briefly as possible it would take too long and our meal is about to be served. So just a few words about the route my unit, the Mobile Workshop No 2, had to take in order to avoid the trap set up by the Russian Forces. After so many days of evading air attacks, on 17th September, we had no choice but to cross over into a neutral country like Romania, surrender our arms and get "locked up" in a camp. Their locking system was not perfect so about one month later two of us escaped to join many other groups and we sailed to France via the Black and Mediterranean Seas.

"The war in France did not last long, so in June (1940) we had to cross over to Oran, Western Algeria, from Oran by train to Casablanca and from there, by boat to Gibraltar. Then, in a convoy, to Liverpool where we landed on 12th July."

Questions started flying about so I lifted my hand and added:

"I am hoping to put all this on paper one day but in the present situation I am not sure whether I am going to write it in Polish or in English. We have to wait for Stalin to stop dictating what shape the future geo-political Europe should be."

Our meal lasted longer than expected and the guests started wishing us a "Good Night" and disappearing, one by one. Alan came to us to explain that tomorrow he would like to start rather early to be able to visit his shop in Lancaster before half-past ten if possible. This meant breakfast at eight o'clock and packing tonight.

Next morning I had only a minute to say "bye, bye" to my lovely girl and beg for her address with a promise of letters as soon as I could get back to my squadron. We set off well before nine o'clock as Alan wished. About a mile down the road I had a chance to wave a

"Cheerio" to the memorable Peel Island and soon after that we were passing Nibthwaite, which meant that there would only be Lake Windermere to say "See you again you lovely lakes".

Not long after that, before we passed Backbarrow, I started feeling a little uncomfortable. "Have I consumed my breakfast too quickly?" I asked myself. The discomfort persisted and by the time we reached the A6 I felt a sharp pain in my abdomen. Passing Carnforth, I couldn't help being restless and uttering slight moans, which of course, attracted Alan's attention.

"What's the matter Waldek?" he asked

"I don't really know, but my tummy is bothering me." I answered. The pain was increasing and I couldn't help groaning louder. Entering Lancaster I had to put both hands on my tummy, it felt as if it was going to explode! Alan was very alarmed by all this and said:

"I am not stopping at the shop. We are going home."

When we arrived at Cartref I could hardly move and Alan had to almost carry me out of the car. Norah must have heard us arrive and when she saw Alan struggling with me she dashed out shouting: "What's happened?" and grabbed my other arm to keep me upright. Together they struggled to get me into the front room and sat me down on the settee but I just slid into a lying down position. Alan called the doctor who arrived very quickly. The doctor diagnosed appendicitis and made arrangements for immediate transfer to the hospital where the diagnosis was confirmed and I had to undergo an emergency operation.

(Now - was this Cupid's method of making sure that this young Polish Officer wouldn't run away too fast? After all, he knew that this young man had spent six months in France and five years on R.A.F.

stations - never far away from young females, so in what state was his "appetite"?)

My friends would not leave me lonely in the hospital and I had many visitors - starting with Norah and Alan, then Jack and Vin and on one day I felt I was being officially assessed by Dorothy's Mother and Auntie. Norah brought them to see me. As they were departing I heard Norah inviting them for a cup of tea. To me it all appeared as a well-organised meeting of "judges" expected to produce an urgent verdict on the subject of "that Polish Officer in the hospital." Their verdict must have been kind to me because within two days I had my first letter from My Darling.

About 10 days later I was released from the hospital to report to my squadron in Silloth. There I received instructions to transfer to Harewood House where my convalescence was to last until May 12th. By May 8th I felt fit enough to take a very modest part in the V.E. Day celebrations.

My convalescence was followed by two postings within three months and on 20th of July I found myself in Kinloss (north-east Scotland) a very long way from Barrow-in-Furness where My Darling lived. The next most important event in 1945 was the V.J. Day on 14th August. At last life could start becoming more normal and without constantly "glancing over my shoulder."

Somehow, with our regular correspondence and occasional few days of leave, we felt as close as conditions allowed. Such conditions persisted for the next 26 months, or for about 760 days. Each single day was a cruel day for my heart.

Dorothy in her nursing uniform, c.~~1964~~ 1944

Now - I feel that this would be the most suitable point where I could add a few words about our "regular correspondence".

Much, much later...actually 58 years later, after My Darling died, I found two boxes and three packets of letters!

240 OF THEM!!

The Sweetheart saved them all without mentioning about it to me until a few weeks before she...left me...all alone...

But let's go back to August '45 and to the events leading me to the day when I would have to consider the most important decision in my life - not in my war activities - but relating to the rest of my life. The question I would like to see answered was: am I free to resign from my profession? After all by now I had risen to the rank of Captain in the Polish Air Force. Would I have to wait for my Head Quarters' decision as to whether we were to return to Poland as an Air Force Unit...or simply stay here or emigrate to any country that would accept us?

Orders to return to Poland would most certain' greeted with a revolt in our units after the news about Stalin's t. of Polish Officers in his mass murder camps like Katyn and other

Whilst we were struggling to find an acceptable answ lives in the future, Mr Churchill, the British Prime Minister, issu most welcome invitation:

"Stay in this country or any country of the British Empire and be treated like our own men!"

At the same time a variety of courses were started to give us some preparation for choosing the right employment. This required a lot of time as well as a variety of postings to stations like Kinloss, Framlingham, Silloth and so on.

By now Christmas of 1946 had passed and both Dorothy and I felt that the time had come for us to make a major decision in our lives. So in March I asked Dorothy to consult with her parents in order that I could have a special meeting with them and formally ask their permission to marry their daughter. Hoping for a positive answer, I asked that they also consider the most suitable dates for them and everybody else for both an engagement party and the Wedding Day. Two days later a letter arrived informing me that the best dates to suit everybody would be the second weekend in April for the engagement party and, about two months later, 21st June 1947 for the Wedding Day.

I applied for and was given a fortnight's leave from the 9th April. So I dashed off to visit Nora and Alan to share my happy news with them. To my great surprise the next day Jack arrived "just for a few hours" as he explained to Norah. But what really surprised me was his invitation for a walk as soon as he had finished his "welcome" cup of tea.

We were strolling along and chatting about nothing particular when suddenly Jack turned towards me and asked:

"Waldek, do you know that Dorothy will not be able to have children?"

I just stopped with my mouth and my eyes wide open, completely dumbfounded, staring at him whilst he continued:

"This is the effect of her illness followed by quite serious operations which the poor girl had to suffer."

I was simply unable to react by saying anything until it struck me that Jack must have been sent as a messenger to give me this terribly sad information and, what's more important, to convey my reaction to Dorothy and to her Parents.

Shaking off the shock, I told Jack:

"I want to marry Dorothy regardless of what you just told me."

By now I was so deeply in love with her that I just could not let Jack go back to them and say:

"I am very sorry but Waldek has changed his mind".

Visualising Dorothy's heartbreaking reaction to such news my heart shrunk violently. After so many of my words expressing love not only in those hundreds of letters or directly to her over the phone, but personally with so many thrilling hugs and kisses.

"OH NO! MY DARLING! I WILL NOT LET YOU GO!! YOU ARE MINE!!!"

So in the end, two years after I found my VALUABLE TREASURE we had a lovely engagement party and two months later, on June 21st 1947

WE GOT MARRIED!!!

We both wanted to have and bring up children so, in due course, we adopted two lovely children: our dear son John and our lovely daughter Vanda.

Our children: Jahn and Vanda at the beach, c.1964

<u>Epilogue</u>

From this very high point in my life I must also try to see the scenery towards the horizons of my life. It looked really promising and even exciting.

Will my wife prove to be as dear and as sweet as her eyes seem to be promising?

I felt compelled to look forward, towards our future, but at the same time I could not stop my mind glancing back into history to find out how it did happen that I am now thousands of kilometres away from my family in Poland. What were the decisive steps that I took or was compelled to take, to come here and feel very happy being "captured" ("...for better for worse, for richer for poorer, 'til death us do part").

Brief analysis of my personal history brought me to the unbelievable conclusion that reaching this climax of happiness was simply due to my good progress in learning English. My progress in English was based on my having to learn languages at school such as Latin, Greek and German. The Classic School was chosen for me by my Parents and my Auntie.

My action in the "Hot War" was badly delayed because the "Cold War" demanded interpreters to help training Polish Air Gunners and Navigators. This delay resulted in my being posted to the Bomber Squadron which, as it happened, was very soon transferred to Coastal Command. The war of this Command was equally "hot" but not with such huge losses. Coastal Command duties required many hours of flying, mainly at night over the Atlantic and the Iceland area.

Now – who would spend many hours on her knees praying and begging The Almighty to help me to survive and to come home safe from any dangerous action? This was my Dear Mother!

So, on my knees, I thank you Mum and anybody who had me in their mind through all the years of the war especially that night when we were attacked by two German night fighters.

I am sure that my Mother wished and prayed that I would return home but if not, that I would find a pretty and loving girl to marry.

oooOooo

Dorothy and I celebrating our golden wedding anniversary – 21st June 1997

Postscript

You may be experiencing difficulties with my name, as have many people before you. 'Waldemar' (or its diminutive form, 'Waldek') is pronounced starting with a 'v' sound to soften the beginning. The same applies to the 'w' in 'Siewruk'. Also, the 'si' sound in Polish is softened to 'sh'. So, if my name was written phonetically it would look more like this: *Valdemar Shevrook* and if you were to vocalise that spelling your pronunciation would be virtually perfect.

Spelling 'Siewruk' also presents people with difficulties. A little "trick" I have shown several British people is as follows. Take a map of the British Isles and lay a ruler across the top of the map. Slide the ruler downwards and you will see that first 'S'cotland is uncovered, then the northern tip of 'I'reland, then northern 'England and finally 'W'ales. The first letters of each spell 'SIEW'. Saying "'R'oyal 'U'nited 'K'ingdom" and taking the first letters of these words neatly completes my surname: 'SIEWRUK'.